Ready, Set, Read!

Other Books
by Jean R. Feldman

Kids' Atlanta

A Survival Guide for Preschool Teachers

*The Complete Handbook of Indoor Games
and Activities for Young Children*

Transition Time

Science Surprises!

Wonderful Rooms Where Children Can Bloom!

Ready to Use Self-Esteem Activities

Ready, Set, Read!

Hundreds of Exciting, Skill-Appropriate, Ready-to-Use Reading Readiness Activities

by Dr. Jean R. Feldman, Ph.D.

Crystal Springs Books
Peterborough, New Hampshire

© 1999 by Crystal Springs Books

Printed in the United States of America

Published by Crystal Springs Books
Ten Sharon Road
P.O. Box 500
Peterborough, NH 03458
1-800-321-0401
FAX: 1-800-337-9929

08 07 06 05   4 5 6 7

ISBN-13: 978-1-884548-28-4
ISBN-10: 1-884548-28-8

Publisher Cataloging-in-Publication Data

Feldman, Jean R., 1947-

   Ready, set, read! : hundreds of exciting, skill appropriate,
ready-to-use reading readiness activities / by Jean R.
Feldman, Ph.D.—1st. ed.
[238] p. : ill. ; cm.
Contents : Teachers Plus! (with Research and Assessment
Tools), Visual Skills, Auditory Skills, Small Motor and Eye-
Hand Coordination Skills, Books and Beyond, Parents Plus!
ISBN 1-884548-28-8
1. Reading readiness. 2. Instructional material. 1. Title.
372.414 -dc21   1999   CIP
LC 99-C74330

Editors: Meredith A. Reed, Cathy Kingery
Cover and Book Design: Soosen Dunholter
Cover Photo: Caitlin Selby
Illustrations: Patrick Belfiori
Publishing Manager: Lorraine Walker

This book is dedicated to

Bonnie and Karl Feldman

Acknowledgments

Special thanks to my parents for reading to me and introducing me to the magical world of literature.

Thanks to Mrs. Myers, my first grade teacher, for so lovingly teaching me to read.

Thanks to Sally, Dick, Jane, Spot, Puff, and Tim. (I still think of them as my friends!)

Thanks to all of my kindergarten and first grade students for their insight on how to teach reading.

And thank you, Wood Smethurst, my amazing and inspiring professor at Emory University, who so generously shared all his expertise and wisdom with me.

Table of Contents

Introduction

Teachers Plus!

Literature Experiences for the Daily Schedule

Assessment

Visual Skills Activities

Auditory Skills Activities

Small Motor/Eye-Hand Coordination Skills Activities

Oral Language Skills Activities

Books & Beyond Activities

Parents Plus! Ideas, Sample Letters, and Activities

Appendix*

*All pages in this section are reproducible.

Ready, Set, Read!

By Jean Feldman, Ph.D.

Introduction

Reading instruction does not begin at some magic age or with a particular program "taught" in schools. Reading is part of literacy development that begins at birth. In a world full of letters and words, young children are naturally curious about what those squiggles and lines mean. All children want to read, but they often lack the prerequisite visual, auditory, and language skills and concepts necessary to succeed. Learning to read is critical to school achievement, as well as life success. The importance of early reading instruction is emphasized by recent research that suggests children who do not learn to read by age 9 will have a difficult time ever catching up.

Helping children become successful readers by developing reading readiness skills and a love for literature requires careful planning and instruction. Children need to be read to and talked with; they need to learn in print-rich environments that inspire the desire to learn. The games, songs, and hands-on activities in this resource book will give children opportunities to develop these readiness skills as they construct knowledge and make meaningful connections. The experience suggested in *Ready, Set, Read!* can easily be adapted for preschoolers to beginning readers.

Section Overviews

Teachers Plus!

This information-packed section keeps you up-to-date with current research findings and information on the ever-evolving discussion on reading. In addition, students and teachers alike will enjoy making the room a comfortable, fun, and colorful print-rich environment with these great ideas. Teachers also will appreciate the creative and informative assessment ideas.

Part 1. Visual Skills

This section focuses on the development of visual discrimination and visual memory skills. Activities progress from students being able to discriminate likenesses and differences in pictures and objects to recognizing their name, letters, and simple words.

Part 2. Auditory Skills

Auditory discrimination and auditory memory skills will be enhanced with the ideas and games in this section. Recognizing common sounds, following directions, and rhyming words will develop phonemic awareness and lead to the ability to identify initial consonants, blend sounds, and decode words.

Part 3. Small Motor/Eye-Hand Coordination Skills

The ability to follow a line of print, left to right orientation, and pre-writing skills will be nurtured through the multisensory experiences in this section.

Part 4. Oral Language Skills

Encouraging children to speak, organize their thoughts, recall information, predict, expand vocabulary, and develop critical thinking skills will be developed and enhanced through these story dramatizations, songs, and props.

Part 5. Books & Beyond

Learn how to set up a wonderful classroom library and writing center in your room. Ideas for class books, big books, bookmarks, story graphs, language experience charts, and extension activities for reading and writing are explored. Teachers and students will enjoy working on these ideas together!

Part 6. Parents Plus!

Home/school activities involve parents in their child's learning and give children the opportunity to reinforce those skills learned at school in their home environment.

Appendix

The Appendix includes:
- Letter Patterns
- Shape Patterns
- Alphabet Pictures
- American Manual Alphabet
- Rhyme Pictures
- Rebus Pictures
- Manuscript Writing Guide

You will appreciate having these resources right at your fingertips!

Teachers Plus!

The Reading Debate

The reading debate is alive and well today as educators continue to argue over the best approach in reading instruction. What is best, you ask? A careful examination of research reveals that no single strategy is best. Clearly, a combination of these approaches is most effective for developing literacy in our schools. Below are the approaches most commonly used.

Whole Word

The whole word approach focuses on memorizing whole words. The advantage of this approach is that children will very quickly experience success and feel like they are "reading." The disadvantage is that they lack the skills to decipher words they don't know.

Phonics

Through phonics, children are taught individual letter sounds that can be blended together to make words. With phonics, children are able to "unlock" words they don't know. However, with so many different sound combinations and exceptions to rules in the English language, phonics can be frustrating for beginning readers.

Language Experience

The language experience approach enables children to see how "talk" can be written down. The teacher writes down what the child says, then he or she reads back over it. Again, children may lack a breadth of skills when this approach alone is used.

Picture Clues and Context Clues

Picture and context clues are also strategies used by beginning readers. Guide children to look at pictures and predict what a story will be about. Context clues enable children to supply an unknown word that makes sense or can be used as a means of self-checking.

Balanced Reading

In recent years, educators have pulled the best from the previous approaches and focused on developing a balanced reading program. With a balanced program, children learn common sight vocabulary and phonetic skills used to decode unknown words. Language experience, reading aloud, shared reading, guided reading, paired reading, independent reading, and writing are blended into a "circle of language" that includes the different strengths and learning styles of all children.

But remember this! Regardless of new reading programs, kits, computer games, or workbooks, an enthusiastic and well-trained teacher is the single most important ingredient in teaching children to read. You are the one who motivates children, encourages them, models for them, and creates experiences where they can interact with oral and written language in an exciting way!

See References on page 25 for books on reading strategies.

Principles of Early Reading Instruction

As you develop a reading readiness program, keep these principles in mind:

- **Follow the child's lead:** Assess each child's level, then plan instruction that will challenge and push him/her to the next level. Build on prior learning and help him/her understand and connect skills.

- **Respect each child's unique learning style and time frame:** Not every child is going to learn to read in the same way at the same time. Learning to read is a continuous process that will evolve as children progress through school.

- **Remember that learning to read is a complex act:** A myriad of readiness skills and social, emotional, and physical factors must be considered.

- **Teach reading in a way that is FUN!** Plan activities where children will be interested and motivated to read and write. Also, help children see the importance of learning to read.

- **DAP:** Use developmentally appropriate practices. Never push or rush children. Use hands-on and open-ended activities where all children can experience success.

- **Include parents in your reading readiness program:** Use workshops, seminars, newsletters, and conferences to connect with parents so they can reinforce learning at home.

- **Teach reading across the curriculum:** Integrate the language arts with meaningful experiences throughout the day. Reinforce important skills by emphasizing written or spoken language in your curriculum and as your students play.

- **Be a good model for children:** Read and write in front of children and demonstrate the enjoyment you get from reading.

- **Learning to read is ACTIVE!** It's not what the teacher does, but the interactions children have with print and books.

Reading readiness should focus on these skills:

- **Visual Skills:** Through visual discrimination skills, children develop the ability to discriminate likenesses and differences in pictures, objects, shapes, and letters. Visual memory skills will enable them to remember letters and words.

- **Auditory Skills:** Auditory discrimination and memory activities develop children's awareness of sounds and lead to the ability to identify letter sounds and decode words.

- **Small Motor Skills:** Multisensory small motor activities will help children follow a line of print and prepare them to write.

- **Oral Language and Concept Development:** Children need ample opportunities to speak and expand their vocabulary. As they develop concepts, they are able to connect with the printed word.

- **Readiness for Books:** A love of books and motivation to read are of prime importance at all levels.

Implications from Brain Research

Recent brain research highlights the importance of early literacy experiences for children (Shore, 1997; NAEYC, 1998). The research also gives insight on developing reading readiness skills more effectively in our classrooms (Jensen, 1996; Wolfe, 1996). Not surprisingly, brain-based learning reaffirms and validates what good teachers of young children have been doing naturally for years!

1. Children need rich experiences that are meaningful and interesting. Only with firsthand experiences do children have something with which to connect learning. Children's brains also enjoy novelty and new things that will challenge and stretch them to the next level.

2. Sensory stimulation and multimedia are critical to learning. The more senses involved in an experience, the more likely children will learn.

3. Children need a safe and secure environment in which to grow. When children feel threatened or frustrated, it is difficult for them to think or process new information.

4. A schedule and routine will enhance learning by reinforcing certain behaviors and helping children know what to expect.

5. Children need caring, consistent relationships. Indeed, interactions with a positive adult are far more important than any piece of equipment or technology.

6. Consider emotional factors involved in learning by nurturing children's self-esteem and celebrating achievement and success.

7. Make sure children have good nutrition and plenty of rest. Take "water breaks" to keep brains hydrated and functioning well.

8. Timing is important. Take "brain breaks," and don't overload children with too much information or too much sitting.

9. Consider your classroom peripherals. Open up blinds to provide more natural light, keep the temperature a little on the "cool" side, use neutral background colors, and arrange seating to encourage social interaction.

10. Children's level of interest is of prime consideration. Children learn through play, so create games and center activities where children will want to go. Remember that learning is a social experience during which children should be encouraged to talk and interact with friends.

11. Children learn through wholeness, so avoid teaching isolated facts. Connect reading and writing throughout the day and relate both to previous experiences.

12. Talk, talk, talk, and listen, listen, listen. Ask children open-ended questions and engage them in interactive conversations.

13. Read, read, and read some more! Reread stories, tell stories, and encourage children to be "story tellers."

14. Use music to enhance learning. Play a variety of music from classical to jazz. Sing songs through your day to guide children and entertain them during transitions. Use rhymes, chants, and songs to increase children's phonemic awareness.

15. Little ones love to move, so be sure to incorporate movement into learning. "Cross-over" activities are especially beneficial for "unsticking" the brain. (There is a midline down the middle of the body. Cross-over activities are those where you reach from the left side of your body over to the right side of the body and vice versa.) Small muscle activities with play dough, art, and manipulatives further stimulate the brain.

16. Repetition is a key to learning, so provide children with activities where they can repeat experiences. "Spiral back" to previous learning and give children new situations in which to practice skills.

17. Integrate patterns and predictions into language instruction: "How is this story like ____?" "What do you think will happen next?"

18. Use recall to reinforce learning and "summarize" information. Recall frequently by giving children time to talk about what they learned, what they liked best, etc.

19. Use a variety of assessment strategies that focus on what children "can do," rather than what they "can't do."

20. Remember, everyone's brain is unique! As multiple intelligence theory suggests, there are many ways to be talented, and there are many ways for children to be wonderful. Create a "discovery museum" in your classroom so children can develop linguistic skills, in addition to mathematical, spatial, interpersonal, intrapersonal, musical, kinesthetic, and naturalistic talents.

References

Burns, Susan, Peg Griffin, and Catherine Snow, eds. *Starting Out Right*. Washington, DC: National Academy Press, 1999.

Chall, Jean. *Learning to Read: The Great Debate*. New York: McGraw-Hill,1967.

Dorn, Linda, Cathy French, and Tammy Jones. *Apprenticeship in Literacy*. York, ME: Stenhouse Publishers,1998.

Durkin, Dolores. *Getting Started Reading*. Boston: Allyn and Bacon, 1981.

Gardner, Howard. *Multiple Intelligences: The Theory in Practice*. New York: Basic Books, 1990.

Gardner, Howard. *The Unschooled Mind: How Children Learn and How Schools Should Teach*. New York: Basic Books, 1991.

Healy, Jane. *Endangered Minds: Why Our Children Can't Think*. New York: Simon and Schuster, 1990.

Jensen, Eric. *Brain Based Learning*. Del Mar, CA: Turning Point Publishing, 1996.

National Association for the Education of Young Children, International Reading Association. "Learning to Read and Write: Developmentally Appropriate Practices for Young Children." *Young Children* 53 (1998): 30–46.

Shore, Rima. *Rethinking the Brain: New Insights into Early Development*. New York: Families and Work Institute, 1997.

Wagstaff, Janiel. *Phonics That Work*. New York: Scholastic, 1995.

Wolfe, Pat. *Mind, Memory, and Learning: Translating Brain Research to Classroom Practice*. Front Royal, VA: National Cassette Services, 1996.

Literature Experiences for the Daily Schedule

Your program goals, children's age, and school schedule will determine the routine you follow every day. Clearly, reading instruction should not be isolated to a time block, but should be integrated in everything you do. Provide for the following "literacy" experiences as you plan your day:

- **Small Group:** Children interact with the teacher in small groups. Play games, read and re-read stories, practice skills, and dictate stories.

- **Independent Activities:** Children look at books or write in journals. If children want to work with a partner, "paired reading" is another effective strategy.

- **Large Group:** The whole class engages in reading big books, poems, and song charts. A large group can also compose and read over language experience stories.

- **Story Time:** Reading aloud to children is the most powerful way to model the pleasure and importance of reading.

- **Learning Centers:** Children have free choice to read books in the library, experiment in the writing center, or work on the computer. Encourage reading and writing skills by adding these props to other learning centers:

    Blocks: Add a carpenter's apron with paper and pencil for children to draw out plans and make lists of supplies.

    - Add crayons, paper, and tape so children can make signs and labels for their structures.
    - Have children build settings for stories you read. For example, students could build a house for the three bears, a bridge for the billy goats, or a castle for the princess.

    Art: Have children draw or paint pictures about a book you've read.

    - Let them make puppets or other characters from sacks or craft sticks.
    - Add labels or dictated sentences to their drawings and paintings. Make murals or bulletin boards about children's classroom experiences and books they have read.

Manipulatives: Make letters with clay or pegboards.

• Use sensory trays to trace names or letters.

• Make lacing cards of shapes and letters.

Math and Science: Make number books or shape books.

• Display posters about plants, animals, land forms, and other topics you study.

• Provide resource materials (e.g., books, magazines) about topics of interest to children.

• Add paper, pencils.

• Have children match and sort shapes or classify objects and pictures.

Dramatic Play: Provide paper, pencils, grocery list, menus, and other appropriate items.

• Add magazines, books, and printed material to your housekeeping area.

• Encourage oral language with play telephones or a puppet theater.

• Offer dress-up clothes so children can experiment with different social roles.

• Add props so children can act out stories.

Creating a Classroom Library

If you want children to read, then you must create an exciting place for them to read! The classroom library offers a safe place for children to experiment with reading, discover the world of books, and share print with their friends.

Equipment: bookshelves
magazine rack or basket
rug, bean bags, pillows, chairs

Materials: wide variety of books
big books
class books
magazines
books and tapes
listening center or Walkman
catalogs, menus, travel brochures, maps
puppets, stuffed animals
flannel board and felt stories
children's paintings, posters, photographs
paper, pencils
multilingual books, examples of different types of print
sensory books, manipulative books

HINT! Check books out of your public library or purchase inexpensive books at garage sales or thrift stores. Also, ask parents for donations of old books or magazines.

Reading Traps!

Rub a Dub Dub,
How About a Reading Tub?
Paint an old bathtub
and fill it with pillows.

Get Comfortable!
Sofa, stuffed chair, bean bags,
rocking chairs, table lamp.

A Reading We Will Go
Build a tent and fill it with a sleeping
bag, flashlight, and books in a backpack.

Tree House
Build a loft in your room for reading.

Dive In and Read Pool
Fill a plastic pool with books and pillows.

Book Club
Decorate an appliance box
to make a cozy getaway.

Encouraging Emergent Writers

Children will be enthusiastic about exploring writing with all of these props!

Equipment: table, chairs, desk organizer, shoe rack, baskets, or tubs
to hold materials

Materials: variety of paper (colored, lined, tablets, notepads, tracing paper,
  carbon paper, etc.)
pencils, pens, colored pencils, markers, highlighters
blank books, envelopes, sticky notes
scissors, tape, stapler, glue, hole punch
rubber stamps, ink pad, date stamp
stickers, Wikki Stix™
clipboard, magic slate
chalkboard and colored chalk
dry erase board and markers
cookie sheet and magnetic letters
manual typewriter
computer and printer
junk mail, old greeting cards, postcards, calendars, check books,
  magazine inserts
dictionary, word file, class list

Authors' Wall

Wall for displaying children's writing

Author's Desk

Old adult desk or school desk

Around the Room with Print!

Using print in a wide variety of ways in the classroom will enhance children's interest in reading and provide them with daily experiences. Children read pictures before they read words, so use illustrations, symbols, children's drawings, photographs, and pictures from school catalogs on your charts and signs.

 Signs

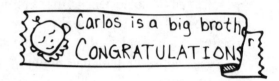

Labels

Charts

Graphs and Calendars

Weather Report

	1	2	3	4	5
☀	●				
☁	●	●			
☂	●	●	●		

March

		◇1	2	◇3	4	◇5
◇6						

Daily Schedule/Highlights

It's Going to be a...
Great Day!

8:00 Sponge Time
8:30 Circle ○
9:00 Small Groups
10:00 Outdoor Play
10:30 Snack 🍎
11:00 Music ♫

Monday, May 2nd
Today's Specials

★ Book about Arthur
★ Water play outside
★ Science experiment with seeds

Visual Maps/KWL

Apples, Fruits, soft drinks, Candy, Junk, Chips, Food, Beef, Meat, fish, Milk, ice cream

Food

Know	Want to know	Learned
food is good need food to grow	how to get stronger	we eat roots and stems

Language Experience Charts

A Special Guest

Joey's dad came to see us.

He is a forester.

He helps protect our trees.

What's bugging You?

Fran- My big sister.

Tim- The dog next door.

Zack- When my mom yells at me.

Bulletin Boards

Rhymes and Songs

The Wheels on the Bus

The wheels on the bus
go round and round,
Round and round,
Round and round.
The wheels on the bus
go round and round

Autumn Leaves
Red leaves
Orange leaves
Yellow leaves
Brown
Twirling Leaves
Dancing Leaves
All fall
Down!

Directions

Make a Snake

1. Get a paper plate.
2. Color it with crayons.
3. Cut in a spiral.
4. Hang up your snake. Ssss!

Funny Faces
You will need:
Crackers
raisins
peanut butter

Directions:
1. Wash your hands.
2. Spread peanut butter on the cracker.
3. Make a funny face with raisins.
4. Eat it.

Assessment

There should be an integral relationship between assessment and instruction. Assessment should guide planning, help you identify individual problems, and enable you to give additional support and extension activities for the children in your class. Assessment should always involve the TOTAL child by including physical, emotional, social, and intellectual development. Assessment should also be authentic and should reflect classroom experiences and program goals. Below are some different strategies that should be utilized when assessing young children.

Observations: Make anecdotal records as children interact in learning centers and play with different materials and games. Use sticky notes that you can transfer later to the child's folder, or use a comment sheet similar to the one on the following page.

Portfolios: Create a portfolio for each child with work samples, drawings, stories, interest inventory (page 39), and other items suggested on page 37. Videos and tape recordings of children speaking or reading are additional media that can be used to monitor children's progress.

Parent Conferences: Use parent conferences as a means of gaining information about children and their experiences with literacy at home. Send home the questionnaire on page 38 to focus on children's interests and needs prior to a conference.

Checklists: Use a checklist similar to the one suggested on pages 40–44 to keep an ongoing record of skills children master or areas where they need additional work. Update frequently to make instruction more relevant and effective.

Classroom Observation

Date: _____

Skills or Concepts: _____

_____

Children's Names   **Comments**

1. _____

2. _____

3. _____

4. _____

5. _____

6. _____

7. _____

8. _____

9. _____

10. _____

11. _____

12. _____

13. _____

14. _____

15. _____

Portfolio

DIRECTIONS:

At the beginning of each month give children a grocery sack and ask them to decorate it with their picture and a sentence. (For younger children, the teacher will need to write the month and a sentence the child dictates.) As the children complete different projects during the month, file their samples or work in their sacks. Examples might include self portraits, writing samples, drawings, art work, paintings, photos, anecdotal records, books read, interest survey, reading log, cutting and pasting samples, journal entries, etc. At the end of the year give each child a blank sack to decorate for their cover. (A photograph can also be used on the cover.) Put the sacks in order, hole punch, and tie them together with string or yarn.

ADAPTATIONS:

Use these books at your end-of-year conference with parents.

Clasp envelopes can also be used to make portfolios for the children. Simply have the children decorate an envelope each month and save samples of their work. At the end of the year, punch two holes in each envelope and put them together with book rings.

HINT! Store paper sacks in a plastic milk crate with the open end up. Print each child's name near the opening so it can be seen.

Use a date stamp to date samples of work.

Materials:
- large paper grocery sacks (10 for each child)
- crayons
- markers
- pens
- pencils
- art supplies
- hole punch
- yarn
- string

Parent Conference Questionnaire

Please complete the statements below and bring this with you when you come for our conference. I'll look forward to the insight you will share with me on your child.

Child's Name _____ Date _____

1. My child's favorite activity at school is _____

_____

2. My child expresses concern about _____

_____

3. My child's positive qualities are _____

_____

4. Areas I feel my child needs to work on are _____

_____

5. Books my child enjoys reading at home are _____

_____

6. Activities my child likes at home are _____

_____

7. I would like to see my child learn how to _____

_____

_____

8. Is there any special information about your child that you think we should know about?

_____

_____

Teachers: Send home a list of multiple intelligences with a brief description of each. Ask parents to read over the list so they can discuss areas that they perceive to be their child's strengths.

Interest Inventory!

Name_____   Date_____

My favorite things to do are . . .

My special friends are . . .

My favorite book is . . .

A song I like to sing is . . .

I am working on . . .

My favorite center is . . .

This is a picture of me doing what I do best . . .

Early Literacy Skills

Note: This checklist represents a continuum of reading readiness skills from preschool through first grade. The activities recommended can be used to instruct and/or assess children.

Visual Skills

Visual Activities

Matches like pictures, colors, shapes, objects	46, 47, 49, 57
Matches objects and shapes with outlines	48
Recognizes and names colors	50, 51, 57, 214
Recognizes and names shapes	56, 57, 124
Matches and recognizes first name, last name	65, 66, 67, 68
Identifies details in a picture	58, 59, 60, 61, 63
Sequences a series of pictures	62
Recognizes labels and signs in the environment	53, 54, 55, 182
Names uppercase letters	69, 70, 71, 72, 74, 75, 78, 79, 184, 202, 203, 204
Names lowercase letters	69, 70, 71, 72, 74, 75, 78, 79, 202, 203, 204
Recognizes the difference between letters and words	89, 92, 153
Tracks spoken and written words one-to-one	50, 122
Identifies high frequency words	81, 84, 87, 88
Reads simple sentences	89, 90, 91

Teachers: If children have difficulty with simple visual and auditory activities, refer them to a specialist for screening.

Auditory Skills

Auditory Activities

	Activities
Listens to stories	173
Listens to and follows directions (two-, three-, four-step directions, etc.)	97
Identifies common sounds in the environment	61, 94, 95
Recognizes sounds (loud, soft, high, low)	95
Identifies rhyming words	102, 103, 111, 112
Discriminates same and different sounds in words (e.g., fan-fan; tan-tin)	98
Repeats words, songs, rhymes, finger plays	100, 101
Recognizes and repeats a pattern	99, 118
Says full name, address, phone number, birthday	156, 194
Makes letter/sound associations	100, 104, 110, 216, 217
Blends sounds to make words	99, 113
Identifies initial consonant sounds	105, 106, 107, 108, 109
Identifies final consonant sounds	109
Distinguishes syllables in words	99

Small Motor/Eye-Hand Coordination Skills

Small motor

Skill	Activities
Stacks blocks	121
Works puzzles	120, 130
Uses a variety of art materials (e.g., paints, crayons, play dough, paste)	125, 130, 143–148
Pretends to "write"	132, 133, 134, 137
Holds pencil correctly	132
Cuts on a given line	131
Traces dotted lines to make shapes	124, 126
Copies square, triangle, rectangle, square	127, 129
Draws simple objects (e.g., person, house, etc.)	137, 140
Demonstrates left-to-right directionality	116, 117, 122
Demonstrates top-to-bottom orientation	123
Prints first name, last name	135, 136
Writes uppercase letters	128, 129, 133, 134
Writes lowercase letters	128, 129, 133, 134
Attempts to write using invented spelling	138, 139, 140, 141, 181, 185, 187
Writes a complete sentence	140
Identifies punctuation (e.g., period, question mark, exclamation point, comma)	142

Oral Language

Oral Language

Activities

Verbally identifies objects	154, 183
Speaks in complete sentences	150
Answers questions in complete sentences	180
Communicates with classmates and teachers	173
Uses language to describe experiences and feelings	152
Dictates related sentences about an experience	152, 153
Uses proper syntax (e.g., plurals, tense)	92
Repeats rhymes, chants, poems	100, 101
Identifies opposites	158
Separates fact from fantasy	177
Demonstrates knowledge of positional prepositions (e.g., over, under, on, off, etc.)	157, 191
Demonstrates knowledge of time (e.g., before, after, tomorrow, etc.)	62
Names objects in a given category (e.g., animals, food, clothing, etc.)	159
Supplies the missing word in a sentence or story	155
Tells a story suggested by a picture or prop	151

Readiness for Books

	Activities
Demonstrates interest in being read to	173, 176, 177, 186, 205–206, 210, 215
Pretends to "read" a book	173, 195, 199, 220
Demonstrates how to turn pages in a book	175
Points out top, bottom, front, back of a book	175
Follows a line of print from left to right	50, 122
Identifies title, author, and illustrator of a book	174, 179
Recognizes parts of a story (e.g., characters, setting, problem, solution)	178, 179
Demonstrates comprehension by answering questions about a story	178, 180
Retells a story in sequence	163, 165, 167, 170, 180, 188, 197
Dramatizes a story	160

VISUAL
SKILLS

Fronts and Backs

Skill:
matching (using environmental print)

Materials:
- empty cereal boxes or food boxes
- scissors

DIRECTIONS:
Cut the front and back panels off the boxes. Lay them out on the floor or on a table. Challenge the children to match up the correct fronts and backs. Can they read the labels on the boxes? Increase the number of boxes that you use in this game as the children's skills improve.

ADAPTATION:
Play a concentration game with the boxes to improve visual memory skills. Spread out the boxes randomly on the floor or a table, then turn them face down. Let one child at a time turn over two box tops. If they match, the child may keep the pair and have another turn. If they do not match, the child turns them back over and another child gets a turn.

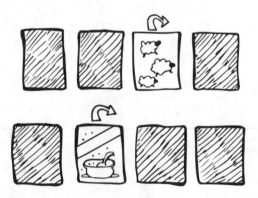

Mix and Match

DIRECTIONS:

Place one of each object in the bottom of each section of the container. Have children sort the objects that are alike and put them together.

ADAPTATIONS:

Write a different letter on the bottom of each section of a muffin pan. Give children pictures that begin with these sounds to sort into the sections.

Write a color word in each section of the muffin pan. Have children sort small toys, crayons, and objects with the appropriate color.

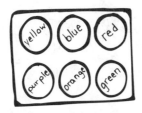 

Bring in a collection of socks (women's, men's, children's, infants', etc.). Put them in a basket and mix them up. Have children match up the pairs that go together.

Get doubles of paint chips from a hardware store. Cut them up, then have children match up like colors. (Bathroom tiles, fabric swatches, and carpet samples can be used in a similar fashion.)

Have children sort a deck of playing cards by color or suit.

Skills:
visual discrimination; color recognition

Materials:
- relish dish
- silverware tray or muffin pan
- small buttons
- coins
- pom-poms
- shells
- party favors
- toys
- eating utensils

Shadows and Shapes

Skills:
visual discrimination; memory

Materials:
- common classroom objects (crayon, scissors, book, block, etc.)
- black construction
- paper
- scissors
- poster board
- glue

DIRECTIONS:
Place different objects on the black construction paper and trace around them. Cut out these shapes and glue them to the poster board. Children try to identify the objects from their shapes, then match them up by placing the object on top.

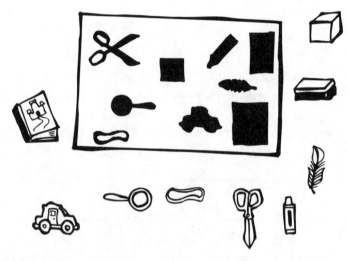

ADAPTATION:
Use attribute blocks or magnetic letters to make a similar game.

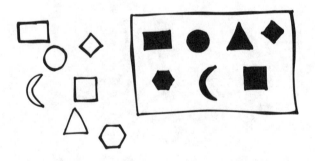

I Spy Bottles

DIRECTIONS:

Fill the bottle two-thirds full with salt or sand. Put five to ten small objects in the bottle and glue on the lid. Lightly shake bottle to distribute objects. Let the children turn the bottle around as they try to identify the different objects in the bottle.

ADAPTATIONS:

Use tinsel, paper confetti, rice, or other materials to hide the toys in.

Take two of each object. Put one in the bottle and glue the other to a piece of cardboard. Challenge children to match up objects on the card with objects in the bottle.

Cut children's pictures from photographs and put them in a bottle. (Include the teacher's and principal's pictures.) Children will be delighted when they recognize themselves and their friends as they shake the bottle.

Skill:
visual discrimination

Materials:
- clear plastic bottle
- sand or salt
- five to ten small toys or objects (crayons, coins, marbles, balloons, paper clips, rubber bands, buttons, etc.)
- glue

Visual

Pointer Finger

Skills:
visual discrimination; color recognition

Materials:
- cotton work glove
- glue gun
- wooden dowel (12" long)
- polyester stuffing
- pipe cleaner
- red marker

DIRECTIONS:

Draw fingernails on the glove with the red marker. Stuff the glove with polyester stuffing. Glue down three fingers and the thumb so the pointer finger is sticking up. Stuff the pointer finger firmly, then put the glove on one end of the wooden dowel. Twist the pipe cleaner around the end of the glove and secure it on the stick with the glue gun. Let one child at a time hold the pointer and find the color sung in the song:

Color Song (Tune: "Muffin Man")

> Oh, do you see the color (color name),
>
> The color (color name), the color (color name)?
>
> Oh, do you see the color (color name),
>
> Somewhere in the room?

Child points to the color with the glove and replies:

> Oh, yes, I see the color (color name),
>
> The color (color name), the color (color name).
>
> Oh, yes, I see the color (color name)
>
> Somewhere in the room.

Continue singing the song as children identify different colors you sing about. Encourage them to name other objects in the room that are the same color.

ADAPTATIONS:

Insert alphabet letters or words in the song for the children to point to. For example, "Do you see the letter *d*?" or "Do you see the word *help*?"

Use the pointer to sweep from left to right under words or sentences.

Have children read big books using the pointer to follow the line of print.

Color Bird

DIRECTIONS:

Use the pattern on the following page to cut a bird out of the front of the file folder. On the file folder, outline the shape of the bird with a black marker, then color a few clouds and trees around the bird as shown. Tape the sides of the file folder together, but leave the top open. Insert the construction paper inside the file folder, making sure that red is on top so you have a red bird to begin the chant below:

> Red bird, red bird,
>
> What do you see?
>
> Here comes another bird.
>
> One, two, three! (Children clap three times.)

Remove the red sheet of paper, then say the chant using the next color revealed in the file folder. Continue until all colors have been named. Put the construction paper back in the file folder, then review the colors. Have children name each color, then point to other objects in the room that are the same color.

ADAPTATIONS:

Use "color bird" to transition children to a new activity. Tell them to watch color bird; they may be dismissed when the bird is the color they are wearing.

Make similar file folders with seasonal shapes (e.g., pumpkin, snowman, heart, butterfly, etc.).

Skill:
color recognition

Materials:
• file folder
• scissors
• colored construction paper cut in 8" x 10" rectangles
• crayons
• markers
• tape

COLOR BIRD PATTERN

Where, Oh, Where?

DIRECTIONS:

Cut out pictures of equipment or toys (e.g., art easel, puzzles, toy cars, sand table, flannel board, etc.) from a school supply catalog. Cut the poster board in 6" squares and glue a picture to each square. Spread the pictures on the floor and ask the children if any of the objects look familiar. One at a time, let a child choose a picture and match it up with the concrete object in the classroom.

Write classroom labels and signs on sentence strips. Have children match up the words on the sentence strips with the labels and signs in the classroom.

ADAPTATIONS:

Hold the pictures in your hand like playing cards. Let children "draw" one, then match up the picture with the real object.

Use catalog pictures to transition children to learning centers. Draw/glue on pictures that represent different classroom centers on cards. Let each child choose a card and go play in that area.

Cut two pictures of similar objects from school catalogs. Glue the pictures to cardboard, then ask children to sort the objects that are alike.

Make a puzzle game where children match up pictures of classroom objects with words.

Skills:
matching; reading labels

Materials:
- school supply catalog
- poster board
- sentence strips
- scissors
- glue

Visual

Labels, Logos, and Coupons

Skill:
matching (using environmental print)

Materials:
- two of each:
  coupons
  labels
- logos (from food products, toys, candy, store sacks, advertisements, etc.)
- scissors
- file folders
- glue
- zipper bag

DIRECTIONS:
Cut out two matching labels, logos, or coupons. Glue one of each on the file folder. Put the other set in the zipper bag. Ask the children to match up the labels in the bag with those on the file folder. Can they read any of the words?

ADAPTATIONS:
Read words on T-shirts or clothing the children wear to school. Copy these words on a language experience chart that you can reread with the children.

Write "We Can Read" on a piece of poster board or classroom bulletin board. Ask children to cut out words they can read from food, toy, and other packages to add to your list.

Let children look through newspapers, magazines, and sale fliers. Underline words they can read with a highlighter.

Walk About

DIRECTIONS:

Make a list of labels and other words in the classroom. You might include the month, center signs, children's names, words on a language experience chart, etc. Photocopy the list and attach the copies to the clipboard. Tie a pencil to one end of the string; tie the other end to the top of the clipboard. Children can "walk about" the room and cross out words as they match them up and "read."

ADAPTATIONS:

Give children a special hat, visor, or glasses to wear when they "walk about."

Put blank paper on the clipboard and have children write their own list of words they can read in the room. Transfer these to a language experience chart and read over the list together.

Let children do crayon rubbings of various labels and signs in the school. Lay paper on top of raised words and rub over the texture with the side of a crayon. (Signs on doors, water meters, and brand names are fun to do.)

Materials:
- clipboard
- photocopy of a list of words in the classroom
- string (18" long)
- pencil

Shape Concentration

Skills:
memory;
shape recognition

Materials:
- poster board cut in 3" squares
- copies of shapes on page 228
- scissors
- glue
- zipper bag

DIRECTIONS:

Make two copies of the shapes. (Color if you desire.) Glue one shape to each poster board square. Place the shapes on the floor or a table and ask the children to name them together. Mix up the cards, then turn them face down. Demonstrate how to play the game by turning over two cards at a time. Name the shapes as you do so. If they match, you may keep them and have another turn. If they don't match, turn the cards back over. The next player takes a turn. The game continues until all shape pairs have been matched.

ADAPTATIONS:

Try using three pairs of shapes to begin this game. Increase the number of pairs as the children's skills increase.

Make other concentration games with uppercase and lowercase letters, rhyming words, colors, pictures and beginning sounds, etc. Stickers can also be used to make memory games.

Here's another game to help children concentrate. You will need three paper cups and one small toy. Turn the cups over in front of you. Place the toy under one cup. Tell the children to watch carefully as you move the cups around. Let a child turn over the cup where he/she thinks the toy is hidden.

Visual

Sack Sort

DIRECTIONS:

Take four sacks and print a different uppercase letter on each sack. Print the same letters on index cards. (Make three cards of each letter.) Set the sacks up on a table. Mix up the index cards. Demonstrate how to play the game by matching letters to those on the sacks and dropping them in. Show the children how to check to see that all the letters are alike when they are finished.

ADAPTATIONS:

Make a simpler game by putting colors on the sacks. Ask children to sort objects of like colors.

Have children sort shapes in sacks.

Make the game increasingly difficult by adding more letters and combining uppercase and lowercase letters.

Have children classify pictures and beginning sounds in sacks.

Use sacks to help children classify objects that are real or pretend; are big or little; are found inside or outside; etc.

Skills:
matching;
classification

Materials:
- paper lunch sacks
- markers
- 3" x 5" index cards or paper cut in 3" squares

Peek-A-Boo Windows

Skills:
memory;
prediction

Materials:
• file folders
• old magazines
  or catalogs
• scissors
• glue

DIRECTIONS:

Cut out interesting pictures from the magazines or catalogs. Glue one picture to the inside of each file folder. On the front of each folder cut a three-sided slit as shown. (Bend the slit so it opens like a window.) Children can open the window on the front of the file folder and try to identify the picture inside. They can then open the file folder to verify their guess.

ADAPTATIONS:

Use children's drawings or photographs in the file folders.

Cut several windows in the front of each folder. The children can open as many as they need to determine what is inside.

Cut circles or other shapes out of the front of a clasp envelope. Insert pictures inside for the children to identify.

Open and See

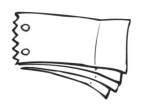

DIRECTIONS:

Take five lunch sacks and fold over the bottom of each sack. Lift the bottom and glue a picture on the sack so part of it will be hidden under the bottom flap. Place the sacks on top of each other, then attach the bags together with brad fasteners as shown. Let the children try to identify each object, then lift the flap to verify their guess.

ADAPTATIONS:

Use pictures from magazines or catalogs to make lunch sack books.

Write children's names on the sacks, then hide their photographs under the flaps.

You can also make bilingual books using this format. Glue a picture on each sack. Write the word in the foreign language on the bottom flap. Open it up and write the English translation as shown.

Picture Picture

DIRECTIONS:

Place a picture on an easel or on the chalkboard in the morning before the children arrive at school. (Don't say anything about it.) When children have gathered for circle time or a group activity, simply turn the picture over and ask, "Who can tell me something they saw in the picture?" When all responses have been made, turn the picture back over and talk about it in detail. Encourage children to keep responding by saying, "Who else can tell me something about the picture?"

Put a different picture up in the room the next day. At circle time, turn the picture over and ask who remembers something in the picture. Use different pictures each day to encourage children to focus on details in a picture.

ADAPTATIONS:

Give children a small, clean paintbrush and have them "paint" the details as they distinguish them in pictures.

Have children look at pictures in books or magazines. Have them make up stories from these pictures. Ask these questions: "What do you think the people are saying?" "What do you think happened before the picture was taken?" "What do you think will happen next?"

Memory Walks

DIRECTIONS:

Tell the children that you are going to take them on a "memory" walk and that their eyes are going to be like cameras. Encourage them to focus their eyes and remember everything they see. After taking the children on a short walk around the school playground, return to the classroom and have them name all the things they saw. Write down their responses on the chart paper. Read over the list together when all the objects have been named.

> 👀 walk
> trees
> children
> cars
> squirrel
> dirt
> rocks
> grass

> 1. birds
> 2. insects
> 3. wind

On another day, take the children on a "listening" walk. Explain that their ears will be tape recorders and they should try and remember everything they hear. When you return to the classroom, have the children recall all the sounds they heard.

ADAPTATIONS:

Have children draw pictures of all the things they see or hear on memory walks.

Teach the children the "Memory Touch" game. Tell them that you have a new game for them to play where their eyes will have to be like a video recorder and remember things. Explain that one person at a time will get up and touch an object in the room. The next person will get up and touch what the first player touched, plus another object. The third player will get up and touch what the first person touched, what the second person touched, and a third object. The game continues with each person touching what the previous players touched in sequential order, plus an additional item at the end. When someone misses, just begin the game all over again.

Skills:
memory;
sequencing

Materials:
• chart paper
• markers

Visual

Order, Please

Skill:
sequencing

Materials:
- camera
- film
- language experience chart markers
(You can cut pictures from school supply catalogs of children engaged in various activities if you don't have access to a camera.)

DIRECTIONS:

Take photographs of children throughout the day at different activities ahead of time: circle time, singing, playing outside, working in centers, eating, resting, listening to a story, and other daily routines. Have the children describe the school day in sequential order. Ask leading questions, such as: "What is the first thing you do every day when you arrive at school?" "What is the next thing you do?" "What comes after that?" Write down the events as the children say them on the language experience chart. Spread the photographs out and let the children put the pictures in sequential order to show their daily schedule. Turn the pictures over and write numerals on the back to indicate the correct order. Mix the pictures up, then let children take turns arranging them. Have them "self check" by turning the pictures over.

ADAPTATIONS:

Put this game in a learning center so children can play it independently.

Make a daily schedule to go on your door. Use the photographs or let the children illustrate it.

Create other visual sequencing games of how children get dressed for school, how a flower grows, how to make a snack, etc.

Take old, torn-up books and cut them apart to make visual sequencing games.

Cut up comics from the funny papers for children to put in order.

HINT! After reading stories to children, encourage them to recall events in sequential order.

Missing Monster

DIRECTIONS:

Cut out the monster parts from felt using the patterns on the following page. Store the pieces in the zipper bag. Place the pieces on the flannel board to make a monster. Tell the children to "take a picture" of the monster with their eyes. Turn the board around and remove one of the parts. Show the children the monster again and ask them if anything is missing.

Skill:
memory

Materials:
- felt
- felt scraps
- scissors
- flannel board
- zipper bag

ADAPTATIONS:

Remove two or three pieces at a time to make the game more difficult.

Let children take turns removing parts of the monster. Have their friends try and guess what is missing.

Play "switch." Switch body pieces around, then have children come up and place pieces in the correct order.

Draw pictures on the chalkboard, overhead, or dry erase board, but leave out some obvious details. Let children take turns filling in what is missing on the object.

HINT! Make a simple flannel board by covering an old game board with felt.

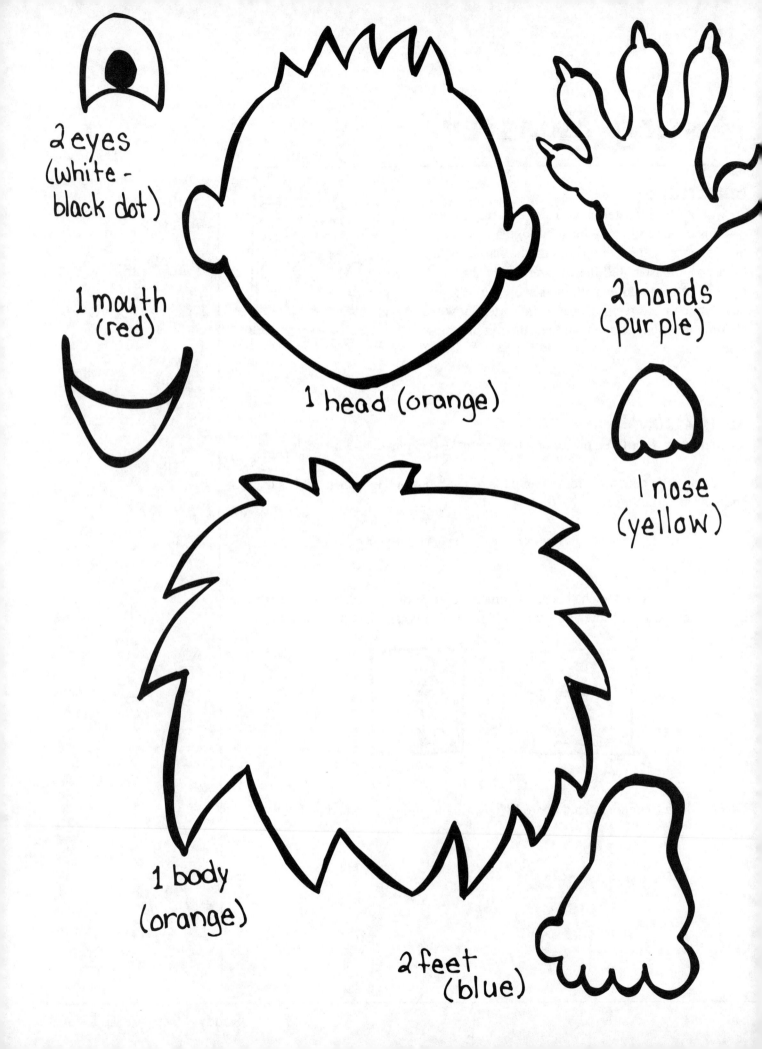

2 eyes
(white –
black dot)

1 mouth
(red)

1 head (orange)

2 hands
(purple)

1 nose
(yellow)

1 body
(orange)

2 feet
(blue)

Name Games

DIRECTIONS:

Print each child's name on an index card, then place the cards in a small box. Choose one child's name at a time and sing their name in the song below.

Name Song (Tune: "If You're Happy and You Know It")

> If your name is (child's name), clap your hands.
>
> If your name is (child's name), clap your hands.
>
> If your name is (child's name),
>
> If your name is (child's name),
>
> If your name is (child's name), clap your hands.

Continue singing the song as you select different children's names. Change motions to "stomp your feet," "snap your fingers," "nod your head," "jump up and down," etc.

ADAPTATIONS:

Let younger children choose an animal sticker to place by their name. This will help them with name association. After some repetition, make new cards with just their names.

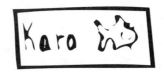

To dismiss children to line up for recess or to go to a learning center, pull one name at a time out of the box.

Choose one child to be a helper for snack each day. Let the "helper" place a name card at each seat. The other children have to recognize their name and sit in that spot.

HINT! Laminate the name cards or cover with clear contact paper to make them more durable.

*Be sure to model correct writing (see page 238). Capitalize only the first letter of each child's name.

Skills:
name recognition; following directions

Materials:
- small box
- index cards

More Name Songs

Skills:
name recognition;
following
directions

Materials:
none

Hello (Tune: "Skip to My Lou")

Hello, _____ (child's name) how are you?

Hello, _____ (child's name) how are you?

Hello, _____ (child's name) how are you?

Hello, _____ (child's name) how are you?

How are you this morning?

Good Morning (Tune: "Did You Ever See a Lassie?")

Good morning to _____ (child's name),

to _____ (child's name),

to _____ (child's name),

Good morning to _____ (child's name),

Howdy-do to you.

Good Bye (Tune: "Good Night, Ladies")

Good bye, _____ (child's name).

Good bye, _____ (child's name).

Good bye, _____ (child's name).

It's time for you to go.

Jump Over the Candlestick (Tune: "Jack Be Nimble")

Note: Set up a candlestick or block for children to jump over as you sing to them.

_____ (Child's name) be nimble.

_____ (Child's name) be quick.

_____ (Child's name) jump over the candlestick.

Name-O (Tune: "Bingo")

There is a friend that you all know,

And _____ (child's name) is their name-o.

_ _ _ _ _

_ _ _ _ _   (Spell out the child's name to the beat.)

_ _ _ _ _

And that is his/her name-o.

ADAPTATION:

After children recognize their first names, make new cards with their first and last name.

Who Ate the Cookie? (chant)

Who ate the cookie in the cookie jar?

_____ (child's name) ate the cookie in the cookie jar.

Who, me? (child responds)

Yes, you. (class responds)

Couldn't be. (child responds)

Then who? (class responds)

HINT! Take children's name cards and put them in an empty cookie box. Pull out one name at a time and use it in the chant.

Name Puzzles

Skills:
name recognition;
small motor

Materials:
• sentence strips
• markers
• scissors
• envelopes

DIRECTIONS:
Write each child's name on a sentence strip. Cut between the letters in their name to make a puzzle. Put the puzzle pieces in an envelope, then print the child's name on the cover. Challenge children to turn the envelope over and put their puzzle together without looking at their name. They can check it by turning over the envelope.

ADAPTATIONS:
Store name puzzles in a shoebox, then let children put their friends' puzzles together.

Make puzzles with children's first and last names. Print their full name on a sentence strip, then cut between words in a puzzle shape.

Make similar puzzles to reinforce sight words. Put picture clues on the front of envelopes.

Using letter stencils, trace letters of the alphabet. Cut out two copies of the letters in each child's name from construction paper. Cut poster board in 9" x 12" rectangles. Glue one set of letters in each child's name on the poster board. Place the other letters in an envelope. Children take the letters from the envelope and match them up to those on the poster board.

Classroom ABC's

DIRECTIONS:

Draw a border with markers around the outside of each square. Print an uppercase and lowercase letter in the upper left hand corner of each card. Glue the corresponding object in the middle, then let a child write the word for the object as shown. Hang in the classroom and refer to letters as you sing songs, review sounds, etc.

ADAPTATIONS:

Make a similar classroom alphabet using environmental print or children's photographs.

HINT! When introducing letters to children, point out similarities and differences in letters. Talk about size, straight lines, curves, "tails" (letters that go below the line), and so forth.

Skills:
letter recognition; letter/sound association

Materials:
- white poster board cut in 8" squares (26)
- markers
- glue gun
- small objects starting with different letters of the alphabet (e.g., plastic apple, block, toy car, dog, plastic egg, artificial flower, etc.)

Letter Cards

Skills:
letter recognition; letter/sound association

Materials:
- poster board cut into 7" squares (26)
- markers
- copies of letters, pictures, and signs on pages 226, 229, and 232
- scissors
- glue

DIRECTIONS:

Outline the border of each square. Glue a letter and the sign for the letter on the front of the card. Glue the picture that represents the sound on the back. (Color in the letters and pictures if you desire.) Use these cards to play one of the games below:

• **Pick Up** Have children stand or sit in a circle. Place the letters face up on the floor in the middle of the circle. Ask two or three children to stand up and call out a letter. The object of the game is to see who can be the first one to find the letter and pick it up.

ADAPTATION:

Use only a few letters when you begin playing this game. As children become more proficient, divide them into two teams to play.

• **Give Me an A!** Hold up cards one at a time as you do this chant.

Teacher shows letter and says:	"Give me an *A*."
Children respond:	"*A*!"
Teacher turns card over and says:	"Apple"
Children respond:	"Apple!"

ADAPTATION:

Teacher passes out a letter to each child. After teacher says, "Give me an *A*," the child with that letter stands up and shouts, "*A*!"

• **Transition Time** Hold up letters one at a time. Children whose names start with that letter may be dismissed to a learning center or another activity.

ADAPTATION:

One at a time, ask children to identify a letter, make the sign, or think of a word that begins with that sound.

• **Alphabetical Order** Mix up cards, then have children put them in alphabetical order on the floor.

• **Visuals** Display each letter as you sing the "Alphabet Song," make "body letters," perform "Phonercises," etc.

HINT! Enlarge the letters and pictures on a copy machine if you desire. Laminate or cover with clear contact paper to make more durable.

Finger Talk

DIRECTIONS:

Cut apart letter signs. Glue one of each sign in the file folder. Put the remaining signs in the envelope. Demonstrate how to remove the signs from the envelope and match them up with those in the file folder. Encourage children to try and reproduce each sign on their hand and identify the letter.

Skill:
memory (using the American Manual Alphabet)

Materials:
- two copies of letter signs on pages 232-234
- scissors
- glue
- file folders
- envelope

ADAPTATIONS:

Sing the "Alphabet Song" slowly as you make each letter sign.

Use signs to spell out high frequency words.

Have children learn to spell their names in sign.

HINT! Introduce this game using five to ten letters. Increase the number of letters as the children's skills increase. Eventually make a game with all 26 signs on a piece of poster board.

Alphabet Soup

DIRECTIONS:

Trace around the soup bowl pattern on the following page on the front of the file folder as shown. Cut out the center of the bowl and decorate the rest of the bowl with markers. Insert the white paper inside and print the letters below on each sheet inside the bowl. Glue the story to the back of the file folder. Begin telling the story, then remove the paper from the front of the file folder to reveal the different letters as they are mentioned.

Alphabet Soup

Alphabet letters in my soup,	1st page - All letters
I eat them all with one big scoop.	
On Monday I eat ABC.	2nd page - A B C
They taste very good to me.	
Tuesday I'll try DEFG.	3rd page - D E F G
Oh, what fun it will be.	
Wednesday go for HIJK.	4th page - H I J K
I could gobble letters all day.	
Thursday let's try LMNO.	5th page - L M N O
Letters are so good, you know.	
Friday PQR and S,	6th page - P Q R S
Eat them up without a mess!	
Saturday time for TUV -	7th page - T U V
They are yummy as can be.	
Sunday slurp down WXYZ	8th page - W X Y Z
Now my bowl is clean, you see.	
Letters, letters, I want more!	9th page - Blank
Let's go to the grocery store.	

Eating letters all week long makes you very smart and strong!

ADAPTATIONS:

Use the soup bowl to reinforce letter recognition or word recognition. Print individual letters on paper so they will appear in the bowl. Have the children name the letters and make their sound as they are revealed. Sight words can also be written on paper and placed in the soup bowl.

Give children pasta or cereal in the shape of alphabet letters and have them glue them on paper to make their names or other words.

SOUP BOWL PATTERN

Use the pattern to draw a soup bowl on the file folder. Cut out as indicated and decorate with markers.

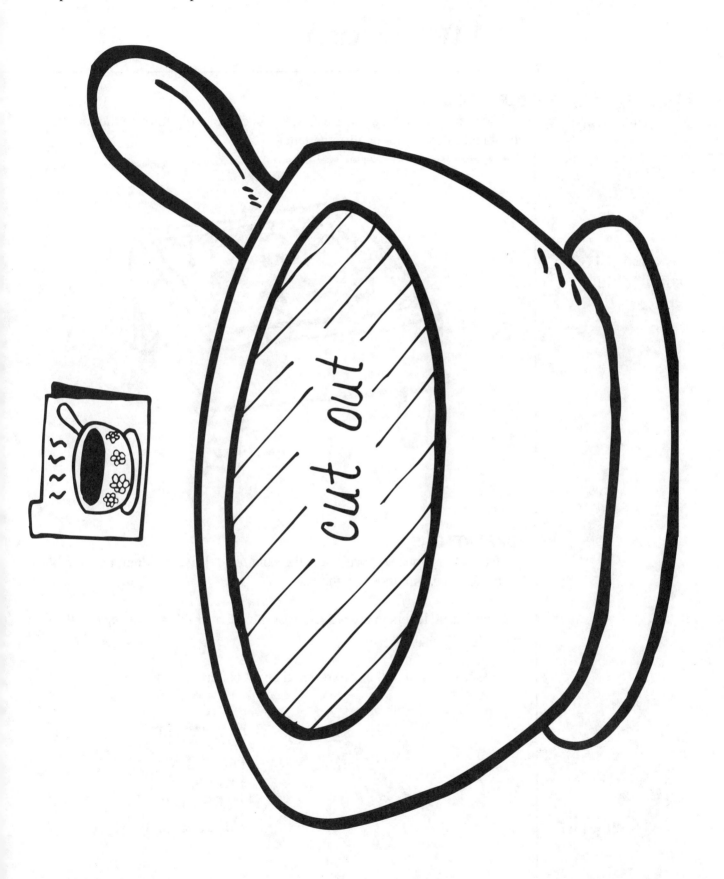

cut out

Letter Hunt

DIRECTIONS:

Hide sensory letters in the sand table. As children dig through the sand and find them, ask them to identify the letters.

ADAPTATIONS:

Hang up an alphabet poster near the sand table. Have children match up the letters they find with those on the chart.

Float plastic letters in a water table or tub. Give children a fish net so they can "scoop up" the letters.

Hide letters around the classroom, then let children "hunt" for them.

Laundry Letters

DIRECTIONS:

Use the patterns on the following pages to trace and cut out 26 shirts and 26 pairs of pants. Print an uppercase letter on each shirt and a lowercase letter on the pants. (Coordinate uppercase and lowercase letters on like colors to make the game easier.) Tie the string between two chairs to make a clothesline. Spread out the shirts and pants on the floor. Demonstrate how to find uppercase and lowercase letters that go together. "Hang" them on the line with clothespins.

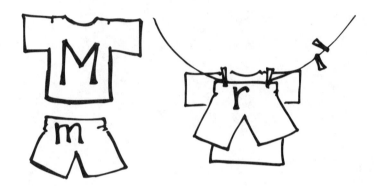

ADAPTATIONS:

Begin with five to ten letters and add more as the children become more confident playing the game.

Have the children hang the letters up in alphabetical order.

Ask children to make words by hanging up lettered shirts.

Make a visual matching game from the patterns. Cut out shirts and pants on like-colored paper, fabric, or wallpaper for the children to match and hang up together.

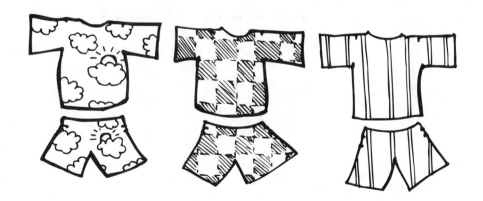

Skills:
letter recognition; identifying alphabetical order

Materials:
- construction paper
- scissors
- markers
- spring clothespins
- string

Visual

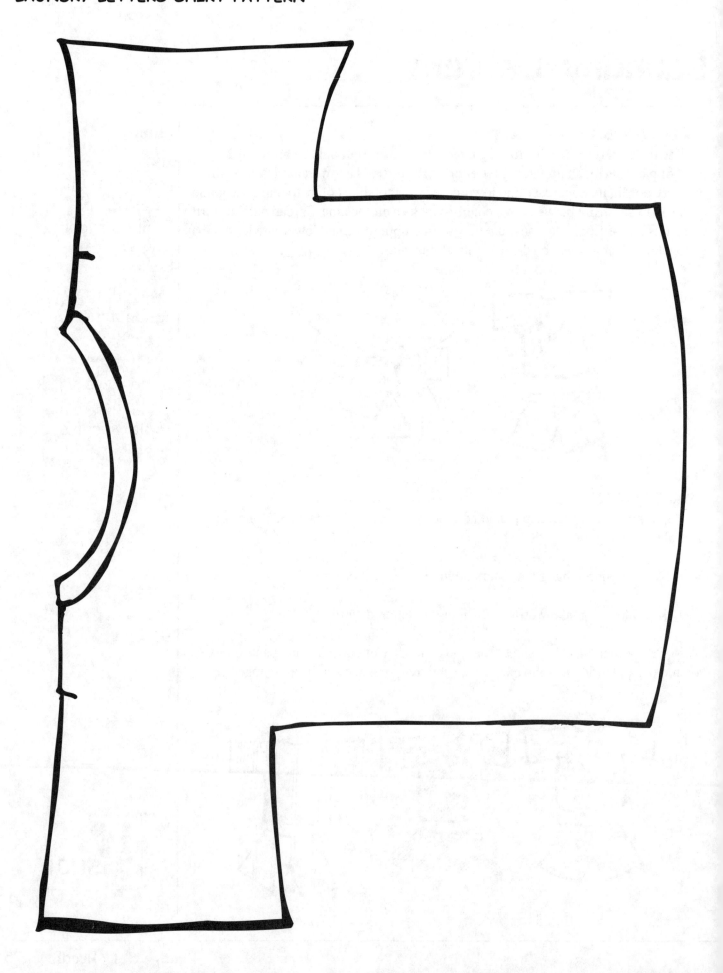

LAUNDRY LETTERS PANTS PATTERN

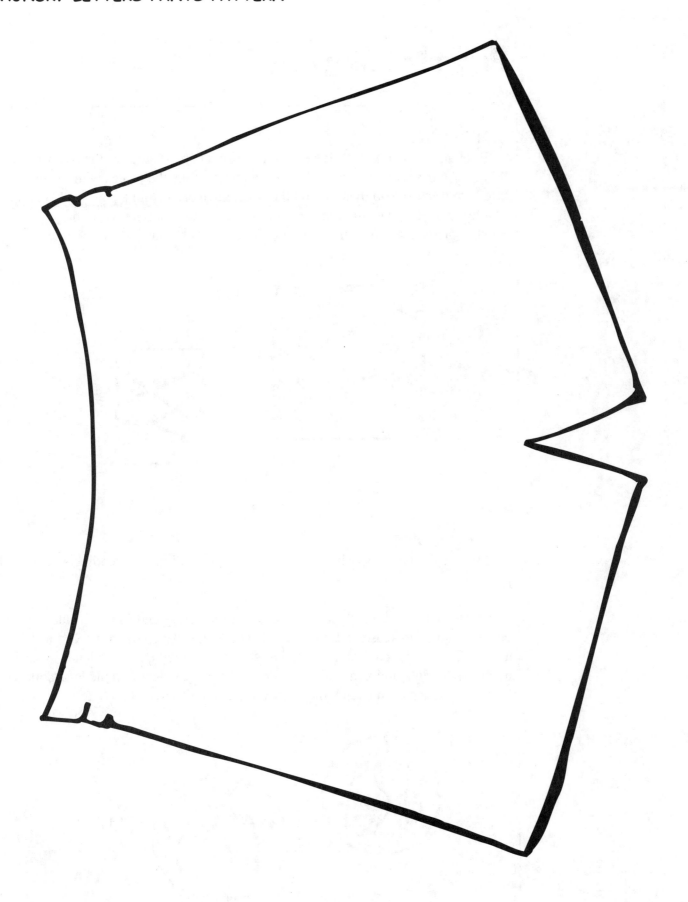

Puzzle Mania

Skills:
letter recognition; matching uppercase and lowercase letters

Materials:
- 26 paper plates
- markers
- scissors

DIRECTIONS:

Print an uppercase and a lowercase letter on opposite sides of the paper plates as shown. Cut between them to make puzzle pieces. Take the pieces with the lower-case letters and spread them out on the floor. Give each child a plate with an upper-case letter on it. Have children stand up one at a time, find the piece that matches theirs, identify their letter, put them together, and sit down.

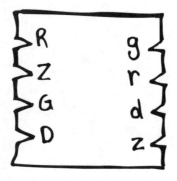

ADAPTATIONS:

Make a similar game where children match up beginning or ending sounds with pictures.

Make stretch and match cards from cardboard scraps and rubber bands to practice matching uppercase and lowercase letters. Cut cardboard into 6" x 8" rectangles. Cut four notches on each side as shown. Print an uppercase letter by each notch on the right and a matching lowercase letter by notches on the left. Children take rubber bands and stretch them between notches to match up letters.

ABC Giant Feet

DIRECTIONS:

Enlarge the foot pattern on the bottom of the page and cut out 26 feet from different colors of construction paper. Print a different letter of the alphabet on each footprint. Tape the letters to the floor in alphabetical order. Cover with clear contact paper. Use the letters to line children up or to transition them to a new activity. You might assign a different letter for each child to find; you could also ask them to stand on the letter that their name begins with, or ask children to name an object that begins with the letter they are standing on.

ADAPTATIONS:

For younger children, use colored footprints. Ask them to find the color that matches what they are wearing and stand on that color.

You can also write numerals on monster feet.

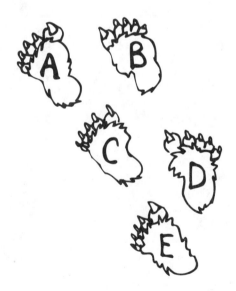

Skills:
letter recognition;
identifying
alphabetical order

Materials:
• construction
  paper
• scissors
• markers
• clear contact
  paper

GIANT FOOT PATTERN

Configuration Station

DIRECTIONS:

Make a copy of the color word puzzle on the following page. Glue the outlines of the words on the file folder as shown. Glue the envelope to the back of the file folder and place the words in the envelope. Explain to the children that people have different shapes, animals have different shapes, and words have different shapes, too. (You might hold up a cutout of various animals to demonstrate this.) Write words similar in style to the ones below on the chalkboard. Outline each word as shown. Encourage children to describe the similarities and differences in the shapes of the words. Show them the file folder game you have made. Have children look at the outlines and guess what color word they think it might be. Let them try different words in the outlines to determine which one fits. Place the game in a learning center so children can do it independently.

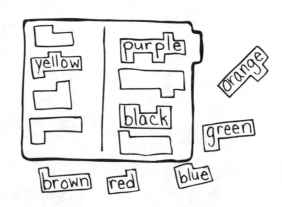

ADAPTATIONS:

Write other words on the chalkboard and have children come up and outline them.

Make similar games where children have to match up high frequency words with their outlines.

Let children make illustrations of words that reflect word meanings. See the samples below.

Skills:
color word recognition; using configuration clues

Materials:
- chalkboard
- chalk
- file folder
- construction paper
- scissors
- glue
- envelope
- copy of color word puzzle on following pages

purple

orange

black

brown

red

yellow

blue

green

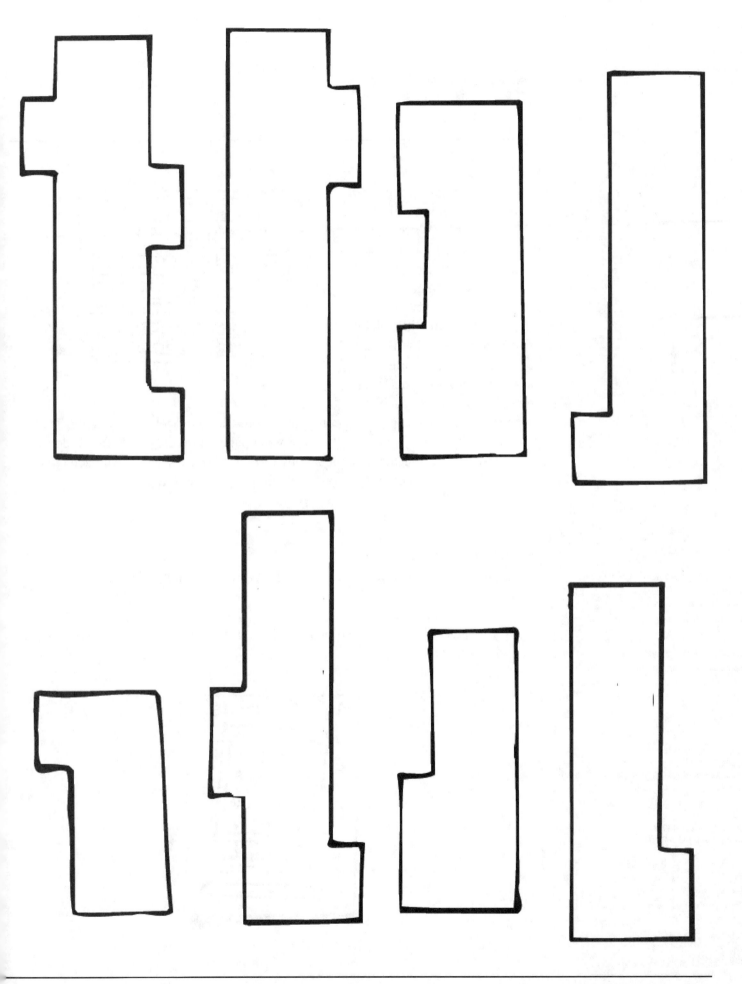

PC Words

Skill:
reading high frequency words

Materials:
- bulletin board
- construction paper
- sentence strips
- masking tape
- file folders
- markers
- crayons
- copy of computer screen from following page
- stapler
- list of high frequency words on page 86

DIRECTIONS:
Make a large computer for your classroom wall similar to the one at right. Write high frequency words on the sentence strips and tape them inside the computer on the wall. Tell the children their brains are like the little chips inside computers that remember things. These words need to be stored in their personal memories. Next, let each child make his or her own "personal computer" word file to use when they write. Trace around the computer outline on the following page on the front of a file folder. Cut out the screen as indicated. Staple a copy of high frequency words for each child inside of the file folder so the words will show up on the screen.

ADAPTATIONS:
Change the list of words in the file folder as the children's sight vocabulary increases.

For younger children, put colors, shapes, letters, or numerals you are working on in their "computers."

High Frequency Word List

a	red	five
I	black	three
in	green	one
like	yellow	four
he	brown	six
go	orange	two
is	blue	am
and	purple	little
work	see	you
run	me	love
mother	up	cat
can	play	jump
help	we	it

* Add words that relate to a unit of study, season, or children's interest.

High Frequency Words

Skill:
recognizing high interest words

Materials:
• index cards
• sentence strips
• markers
• list of words on page 86

DIRECTIONS:

High frequency words are those words that occur often in print. Rather than having to sound them out individually, children will be able to read more fluently if these words are "automatized" (i.e., they "automatically" recognize them when they see them). These words should be used in context and not "drilled." Make up games, use the words in stories, highlight them on language experience charts, etc. On the previous page are suggested high frequency words for beginning readers. Again, choose words that your children are interested in and focus on words when children are READY!

Word of the Day: Introduce a new word each day and add it to a growing list on the wall. Have children use the word in sentences, identify it in books, or point to it in the classroom.

Screen Saver: Put high interest words on your computer screen saver.

Show Me: Place words on the floor or on a table. Call out a word, then choose a child to "show me" and use it in a sentence.

Word Hunt: Pass out books, magazines, or newspapers. Show the children a word, then ask them to find it in print.

Line Up: Pass out a word to each child. When you call out their word, they may line up or move to a new activity.

Games: Use sight words in file folder games and card games such as "Go Fishing," "Concentration," "Bingo," etc.

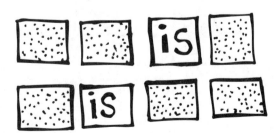

Word Rings

Skills:
reading high frequency words; writing

Materials:
- 3"x 5" index cards
- markers or crayons
- scissors
- glue
- hole punch
- old magazines or workbooks
- photographs
- rebus pictures on pages 236-237
- book ring

DIRECTIONS:

Cut out small pictures of objects familiar to the children, such as animals, foods, places, people, actions, etc. Glue one picture on each index card and write the word beside it. Hole punch the upper left hand corner, then put the word cards together on the book ring. Show the word ring to the children and have them read over the words with you. Explain that you will put the word ring in the writing center. When they want to know how to write a word, they can use the word ring to help them.

ADAPTATIONS:

Make individual word rings for children. Have the children dictate words they want to learn on index cards, then illustrate them. Hang the word rings on a pegboard for easy use.

Use a Rolodex to alphabetize high frequency words. Place in the writing center for children to use for independent writing.

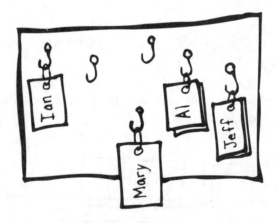

Building Sentences

DIRECTIONS:

Lay a rectangular block on the paper and trace around it to make a pattern. Cut out 12 of these shapes from the paper. Print the words below on the paper rectangles and tape them on the blocks. Cut out the rebus pictures of actions and tape them by the words. Explain that when you put blocks together in different ways you can build different things. And when you put words together in different ways, you can build different sentences. Put out the blocks below one at a time, having the children repeat the words with you.

I	jump	hop
You	walk	skip
sleep	eat	swim
We	can	run

Take three blocks and build a sentence naming each word and sweeping your hand from left to right as you do so. Ask the children to read the sentence with you. Demonstrate how to change the last word to make it say different things. Have the children read the new sentences with you as you create them. (Point out how the picture will help them read the words.) Change the first block to "I" or "You" to make additional sentences the children can read.

ADAPTATIONS:

As the children improve, make additional word blocks for sentence construction.

Let the children act out what the sentences say.

Make a class book called "I Can" where the children draw pictures and dictate sentences about what they "can" do.

Skill:
reading simple sentences

Materials:
• unit blocks
• heavy paper
• scissors
• tape
• markers
• rebus pictures on pages 236–237

Rebus Reading

DIRECTIONS:

Write down sentences children dictate about what they like to do at school on the sentence strips. Use the rebus pictures to illustrate the sentences. Place the sentences in the pocket chart and read over them as you move your finger in a left-to-right direction. Have the children come up and take turns reading the sentence they dictated as they point to each word.

Hole punch sentence strips on the left and attach a book ring to make a book.

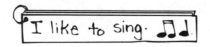

ADAPTATION:

Use the pocket chart as part of your daily routine. Have children fill in the day, weather, number of children present, and so forth.

Secret Message

DIRECTIONS:

Use the white crayon to write different messages on the paper. You can write children's names or affirmations such as: "I like you"; "You're the greatest!"; "Have a happy day!" (Cover a table with newspaper and put out the paints and brushes.) Distribute a secret message to each child. Explain that when they paint over their paper they will be able to read their secret message. Have children read their messages to each other.

ADAPTATIONS:

Let the children write their own secret messages or draw pictures with white crayons on paper. They can trade them with a friend or take them home for their parents.

Use rubber cement to write words or letters on paper. Brush over with paint, dry, then rub off the rubber cement.

Older children may enjoy using this secret code to write messages. Use the numerical symbol for each letter. For example;

9		12	9	11	5		25	15	21
I		**l**	**i**	**k**	**e**		**y**	**o**	**u**

Secret Code:

1 2 3 4 5 6 7 8 9 10 11 12 13 14 15 16 17 18 19 20 21 22 23 24 25 26
a b c d e f g h i j k l m n o p q r s t u v w x y z

HINT! Write messages to children on a classroom mirror with a dry erase marker.

Skill:
reading simple sentences

Materials:
• white crayon
• paper
• diluted tempera (one-third paint to two-thirds water)
• large brushes
• newspaper

Add an Ending

Skill:
recognizing word endings

Materials:
- overhead projector sheets
- permanent markers
- poster board

DIRECTIONS:

Write the following endings on the projector sheets with markers and cut out.

s   ing   ed

Write nouns and verbs similar to those listed below on the poster board. Explain to the children that you can add letters to the end of words to change their meaning. Read the word "book." Explain that if you have lots of them, then you should say "books." Take the -s ending and add it to the end of the word. Continue to read through the list of nouns (adding -s) and have the children tell you what it says.

Next, read the word "jump." But if I say, "I am jump," it doesn't sound right. That's because I need to add "ing" to the end of the word. Continue to go through the list of verbs (adding "ing") and encourage the children to read the words. Follow a similar procedure for introducing "ed."

ADAPTATIONS:

Write endings on 3" circles of cardboard. Tape to Popsicle sticks, then add to the ends of different words.

As you read big books and other classroom print, point out different word endings. Have the children identify the "root word" and the "endings."

Make a language experience chart with words and their endings. Have children underline root words and circle endings.

Make a book with singulars and plurals. Have children fold their paper in half. On one half draw one animal or object. On the other half draw many of the same object. Encourage the children to write labels, and make sure they add the *s*.

AUDITORY SKILLS

AUDITORY
DISCRIMINATION

AUDITORY
MEMORY

PHONEMIC
AWARENESS

REPEATING SONGS
AND CHANTS

RHYMES

MAKING
LETTER/SOUND
ASSOCIATIONS

BLENDING
SOUNDS

IDENTIFYING
INTIAL SOUNDS

Sound Detectives

Skills:
auditory discrimination; memory; phonological awareness

Materials:
- film containers (available free where film is developed)
- rice
- salt
- popcorn kernels
- pennies
- masking tape
- markers

DIRECTIONS:
Fill two film containers one-third full with rice. Put salt in two of the containers, popcorn kernels in two others. Follow with other materials. On the bottom of each container put a small piece of masking tape. Make dots of like colors on the tape of the cans that make the same sound. Spread the containers out in front of the children. Pick up one and shake it. Explain that there is another can with the same thing in it. Tell the children to play detective and see if they can help you find the other can that matches it. Pick up the cans one at a time and shake them until you find the matching pair. Put them together. Continue shaking the other cans until you match them all up. Turn the cans over. The colors on the bottoms should match. Let the children play this game independently or with a friend.

ADAPTATIONS:
Start with two pairs for children who have difficulty discriminating sounds. Add more cans as children's skills improve.

Use paper clips, Styrofoam chips, macaroni, beans, and other common items to make additional sound cans. Distribute one to each child. Have them walk around the room and try to find their sound partner.

Glue samples of what is in each can on a piece of cardboard. Challenge the children to match up the cans with what they think is inside.

You can also put mystery objects in plastic bottles, then insert them in socks. Children shake the bottles and try to identify the contents.

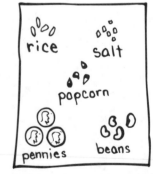

HINT! Glue the lids on with a glue gun to avoid spills. Store the cans in a self-locking plastic bag, basket, or shoebox.

Strike Up the Band!

DIRECTIONS:

Cut the top, bottom, and one side off the box. This will make a three-sided screen that you will need for this game. Place three instruments in front of the children and play them one at a time as you name them. Put the screen in front of the instruments and tell the children to listen and see if they can identify the instrument that you play. Let the children take turns playing an instrument as their friends guess which one it is. Add more instruments to make the game more difficult.

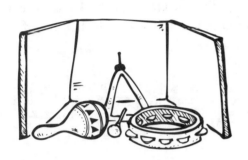
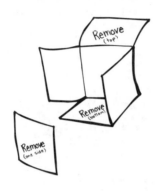

ADAPTATIONS:

Take common household objects, such as a glass, cup, bottle, or can. Strike each one with a spoon, then have the children close their eyes and identify which one you strike.

If you have a xylophone or piano, strike a high note, then a low note. When the children close their eyes, have them identify if you strike high or low notes.

Play some music for the children to move or dance to. When the music stops, they must "freeze." Continue playing music as children listen and stop or start.

Sound Safari

Skills:
auditory discrimination; recognizing familiar sounds

Materials:
• tape recorder
• blank tape

DIRECTIONS:
Make a tape recording of environmental sounds that the children would be familiar with. (Make each selection at least 15–30 seconds long.) Sounds might include a dog barking, fire truck siren, birds singing, water running, car engine, baby crying, musical instrument, kitchen appliance, telephone ringing, etc. Explain that you will play a tape with different sounds. Tell the children to close their eyes and see if they can visualize what is making each sound. Play the sounds one at a time, pausing between selections so that children can discuss what they think it is. Rewind the tape and play it a second time. Tell the children to smile or wiggle their feet if they know what it is.

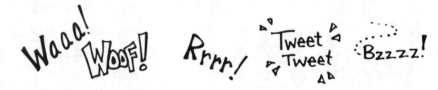

ADAPTATIONS:
Spread out pictures that represent the different sounds on the tape. Have children match up each sound with its picture.

Have each child say a sentence or rhyme on the tape recorder. Play it back for the class and ask them to identify their classmates' voices.

Let children take turns making different environmental sounds as their classmates try and guess what they are.

Let children make sound effects when you read them a story. Choose one or two relevant sounds from the story, such as an animal, siren, type of weather, etc. For example, if there is a lion in the story, the children can "GRRR" every time you read "lion." If there is thunder, they can stomp their feet. They could "BOOOO!" for the villain or cheer "HOORAY" for the hero.

HINT! Purchase an inexpensive Walkman for individual listening activities. Offer children story tapes, classical music, international music, and a wide variety of choices.

Grandmother's House

DIRECTIONS:

Place the food on a table or shelf on one side of the room. Tell the children that the shelf/table is the grocery store. Sit with the children on the opposite side of the room and tell them that you're going to pretend to be "grandmother." Explain that you're going to play a game of memory where they get to go to the "grocery store" to get some food for you. Name several foods, then choose a child to skip across the room with the basket, select the objects named, and skip back to you. Begin by naming two foods, then increase it to three, four, and more as the children's auditory memory improves.

Skills:
memory;
following
directions

Materials:
• basket or bag
• plastic foods or empty food containers (cans, cereal boxes, etc.)

ADAPTATIONS:

Use a book, block, doll, crayon, and other common classroom objects to play this game.

Play "Simon Says" and "Mother, May I?" to encourage children to listen and follow directions.

Play a rhythm echo game. Clap or snap various patterns for children to listen to and repeat.

Make a tape recording of different directions similar to the ones below. Have children listen to the tape and follow the directions in order. For example:

"Stand up and touch your head."

"Turn around, jump, and clap your hands."

Thumbs Up! Listen Up!

Skills:
auditory discrimination; phonological awareness

Materials:
none

DIRECTIONS:

Tell the children they will need their thumbs and ears to play this game. If their ears hear the same sound twice (because you have repeated the word), they should put up their thumbs. If they hear two different sounds, they should put their thumbs down. Hold out your thumbs and demonstrate:

"Meow" —> "Meow"	(Thumbs up)	
"Meow" —> "Oink"	(Thumbs down)	

Use animal sounds until the children catch on. Next use the children's names to play the game:

"Jenny" —> "Jenny"	(Thumbs up)	
"Jenny" —> "Zack"	(Thumbs down)	

Play the game, increasing the difficulty until you are using very similar words:

"Man" —> "Man"	(Thumbs up)	
"Man" —> "Men"	(Thumbs down)	

ADAPTATIONS:

Play the game using rhyming words. If the words rhyme, the children should put their thumbs up. If they don't rhyme, the children should put their thumbs down.

"Cake" —> "Lake"	(Thumbs up)	
"Cake" —> "Bird"	(Thumbs down)	

Use this same technique to encourage children to listen for words that begin with a particular sound. When you say words that start with the same sound, the children put their thumbs up, but when you say a word that does not start with that sound, they put their thumbs down.

"red, rain, rose, ride, book, run, river, ribs" (Thumbs down on "book")

Say nursery rhymes, but transpose letters and mix things up. Tell children to stick up their thumbs when they hear something wrong. For example:

"Jack and Bill went up a hill . . ."

"Hey diddle, diddle, the bat and the fiddle . . ."

Yoohoo, Yoohoo!

DIRECTIONS:

To get children's attention, tell them that you're going to play a game with them where they will be your "echo" and repeat everything you say or do. Begin saying phrases similar to those below:

Yoohoo.   (Give children time to repeat each line.)

How are you?

Explain that words are made up of individual sounds, and when you put the sounds together you can make words. Demonstrate with simple words, such as "cat" (c - a - t) and "dog" (d - o - g).

Next, tell the children you will say the individual sounds. They should blend the sounds together and echo back the word.

Teacher says:	m - a - n
Children echo:	man
Teacher says:	t - i - m - e
Children echo:	time

Make individual sounds as children blend them and make words.

ADAPTATION:

Play the syllable clap game by having children clap out the different syllables or beats they hear in each other's names. Continue by clapping or snapping out syllables in longer words and phrases.

HINT! Say sounds slowly, then tell children to "smoosh" them together to make words.

Tooty Ta Chant

Skills:
phonemic
awareness;
oral language

Materials:
none

DIRECTIONS:

Teach the children the "Tooty Ta" chant below. They should say each line after you and make the motions:

Tooty Ta* Chant

A tooty ta, a tooty ta, a tooty ta ta.   (Children repeat)

Thumbs up.

A tooty ta, a tooty ta, a tooty ta ta.

Thumbs up.

Elbows back.

A tooty ta, a tooty ta, a tooty ta ta.

Thumbs up.

Elbows back.

Feet apart.

> Tooty Ta!
> Tooty Ta,
> Tooty Ta,
> Tooty Ta Ta,
> Thumbs Up!

Chant continues by adding a new body part to each verse.

Thumbs up

Elbows back

Feet apart

Knees together

Bottoms up

Tongue out

Eyes shut

Turn around

Ask children to reproduce the sound that they hear at the beginning of "Tooty Ta." Do they know any other words that begin with that sound? Show them the letter *T* and explain that it makes the sound they hear.

ADAPTATION:

Substitute different consonants in the chant as you learn them. For example, if you are working on *B*, you could do "Booty ba, booty ba, booty ba ba." For *L* you could say, "Looty la, looty la, looty la la," and so forth for the other sounds.

*HINT! Pronounce the *a* with the /ā/ sound.

Next Time Won't You Sing with Me?

DIRECTIONS:

Sing the familiar alphabet song, then try singing some of the creative versions suggested at the bottom of the page.

Alphabet Song (Tune: "Twinkle, Twinkle, Little Star")

A B C D E F G

H I J K L M N O P

Q R S

T U V

W X Y and Z

Now I've sung my ABC's.

Next time won't you sing with me?

Fast:	Sing rapidly.
Slow:	Sing very slowly.
Underwater:	Put your index finger between your lips and vibrate.
Monster:	Stomp your feet and sing loud and slow.
Leprechaun:	Tap index fingers and sing in a high, tiny voice.
Opera:	Extend arms and dramatically sing like an opera star.
Upside Down:	Bend over, put your head on the floor, and sing.
Backward:	Turn around and sing with your back to the group.

ADAPTATIONS:

Clap, snap, tiptoe, and make other motions as you sing.

Have the children make up their own silly ways to sing this song. Point to the letters in the classroom as you sing.

Skills:
memory; learning alphabetical order

Materials:
none

Nursery Rhyme Rap

Skills:
memory;
recognizing and
using rhyming
words

Materials:
none

DIRECTIONS:
Sing nursery rhymes to this familiar tune. Have the children repeat each verse with you.

Nursery Rhyme Rap (Tune: "100 Bottles of Beer on the Wall")

> Jack and Jill
>
> Went up the hill
>
> To fetch a pail of water.
>
> Jack fell down and broke his crown
>
> And Jill came tumbling after.
>
>
> Humpty Dumpty sat on a wall.
>
> Humpty Dumpty had a great fall.
>
> All the king's horses
>
> And all the king's men
>
> Couldn't put Humpty together again.

Sing nursery rhymes such as "Little Miss Muffet," "Rub a Dub Dub," "Hey, Diddle Diddle," "Little Boy Blue," etc., to the above tune. You'll be amazed how many will work!

ADAPTATIONS:
Say different rhymes, but leave off the last word of each line for the children to fill in.

Ask children to tell you the words that rhyme in each verse.

Have children draw pictures of different nursery rhymes. Write the words on the bottom of each page, then put the pages together to make a book. The children can "sing and read" at the same time.

Rhyme Lotto

DIRECTIONS:

Color the rhyming pictures with crayons or markers and cut apart. Divide one piece of paper into a grid with six sections (as shown below). Glue one rhyming picture in each section. Take the other set of rhyming pictures and glue them to another sheet of paper. Cut the pictures apart and store them in the envelope. Demonstrate how to play the game by spreading out the cards. Name the pictures on the game board. Tell the children to listen carefully to the ending sound of each word, then find another picture that ends the same way and put it on top of it.

ADAPTATIONS:

Make several different game boards with other rhyming words.

As children advance, make lotto games using words that rhyme instead of pictures.

Play "roll and rhyme." Say a word, then roll a ball to a child. They must say a word that rhymes as they catch the ball.

Make lotto games on file folders where children can match like shapes, uppercase and lowercase letters, or pictures and beginning sounds.

Skills:
phonemic awareness; recognizing and using rhyming words

Materials:
- heavy paper cut in 9" x 12" pieces
- copies of rhyming pictures on page 235
- crayons or markers
- scissors
- glue
- envelope

The Letter Farm

Skills:
phonemic
awareness;
practicing letter
sounds

Materials:
• 6" x 8" pieces
of poster board
(26)
• markers

DIRECTIONS:

Print a letter of the alphabet on each card. Hold up one letter at a time as you sing:

The Letter Farm (Tune: "Bingo")

There is a letter that we know,

And T is its name-o

T t t t t   (Make a *T* sound)

T t t t t

T t t t t

And T is its name-o.

Continue singing the song using other letters of the alphabet.

ADAPTATIONS:

Have children identify words that begin with each letter as you sing about them.

Here are other songs for reinforcing letters and sounds:

Letter Sounds (Tune: "Old MacDonald Had a Farm")

Ms./Mr. (teacher's name) had a school,

E I E I O.

And in their school they had an "M,"

E I E I O.

With a "mmm" here, and a "mmm" there.

Here a "mmm," there a "mmm," everywhere a "mmm."

Ms./Mr. (teacher's name) had a school,

E I E I O.

I'm Looking for the Letter (Tune: "Go In and Out My Window")

I'm looking for the letter, I'm looking for the letter,

I'm looking for the letter that says, "P-p-p."

(Child comes up and points to the letter *P*.)

Letter Chart

DIRECTIONS:

Select a letter and write it at the top of the page. Ask children if they know the name of the letter. Reproduce the sound together. Ask the children to think of a word that begins with that sound. As each child contributes a word, write it on the chart. Encourage the children to add as many words as they can. Give them hints and riddles about words that begin with that sound. Read over the words together. Choose individual children to come up and underline a word they can "read."

ADAPTATIONS:

Use an overhead projector, dry erase board, or chalkboard to make letter charts.

Hang letter charts on a classroom wall for recall.

Choose a different child to illustrate each letter chart, then let them take it home.

Put these charts together to make a giant book.

Have children cup their hands around their ears as they reproduce sounds.

Pass around a hand mirror. Encourage children to look at their mouth movements as they reproduce various sounds.

Phonercise

Skills:
understanding initial sounds; understanding alphabetical order

Materials:
none

DIRECTIONS:

Have the children stand and follow along with you. To begin this exercise put your arms in the air and say "a." Touch your shoulders and make the short *a* sound. Touch your toes and name something that begins with the short *a* sound, such as "apple." Put your hands in the air and say "b." Touch your shoulders and make the *b* sound. Touch the floor and say something that starts with that sound (e.g., "bubble"). Exercise as you work through the alphabet.

ADAPTATIONS:

Point to the letters on a chart or other display as you say them.

Spell out words using phonercise.

Challenge children to name words in a particular category as you phonercise. For example, they could name just animals, foods, or actions.

Let the children make letters using their bodies, or divide them into small groups to form letters with their bodies.

Locomotion Letters

DIRECTIONS:

Have the children stand and act out the motions below as you name different letters of the alphabet. Say the letter and demonstrate as you emphasize the sound that each letter makes.

A - act (extend arms in dramatic fashion)

B - bounce (pretend to bounce ball)

C - cut (pretend to cut with fingers)

D - dive (hold arms in diving position)

E - eat (pretend to feed self)

F - fly (flap arms as if flying)

G - gallop (gallop in place)

H - hop (hop on one foot)

I - itch (scratch self)

J - jump (jump up and down)

K - kiss (kiss in the air and hug self)

L - leap (leap in the air)

M - march (march in place)

N - nod (shake head)

O - open (open eyes wide)

P - push (extend arms and push)

Q - quiet (put finger on lip)

R - roll (roll hands)

S - sit (sit down)

T - tickle (wiggle fingers)

U - understand (scratch head)

V - vibrate (jiggle all over)

W - walk (walk in place)

X - x-ray (pretend to x-ray hand)

Y - yawn (pretend to yawn)

Z - zoom (brush hands swiftly across each other)

Sing the letters and actions to the tune of "Frère Jacques" as you make the motions: "*a* is for act, *b* is for bounce, *c* is for cut, *d* is for dive," etc.

ADAPTATIONS:

Hold up letter cards as you introduce sounds and motions.

Let the children think of their own words to dramatize for each sound. How many different things can they think of for each letter?

HINT! Children learn through moving, so associating sounds with verbs and movements might be more meaningful than using objects (nouns).

Toss a Sound

DIRECTIONS:

Divide the poster board into a grid with six sections. (Vary the number of spaces and letters used with the ability of your students.) Color and cut out the pictures that represent the different letters. Glue one picture in each section of the poster board. Place the poster on the floor. Let children take turns tossing the bean bag onto the board. Each child then identifies the letter he or she hears at the beginning of the object.

ADAPTATIONS:

Ask children to name another word that begins with the same sound.

Make two different boards by using the front and the back of the poster board.

Put a piece of masking tape on the floor for children to stand behind as they toss the bean bag.

Make similar games to reinforce color recognition, shapes, and letters.

HINT! Make a bean bag by filling the toe of an old sock with one-half cup of dried beans. Tie a knot around the beans, then pull the cuff of the sock back over the toe.

Letter Dice

DIRECTIONS:

Wash out the milk cartons. Cut the tops off to within 3½" from the bottom. Squeeze the top of one carton and insert it into the other to create a cube. Cut six 3½" x 3½" pieces of construction paper (same or different colors). Print a letter on each square, then glue the squares to the sides of the cube. Wrap the cube with clear packaging tape or contact paper to make it more durable. Let the children take turns rolling the die and identifying the letter. Encourage them to reproduce the sound and name a word that begins with that sound.

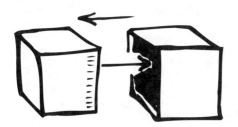

ADAPTATIONS:

Make cubes with blends and digraphs.

Have children think of words that end with letters rolled.

Print words on dice for the children to read and use in sentences.

Take a plastic beach ball or playground ball and write letters on it with a permanent marker. Roll or toss the ball to the children. They must name the letter or say a word that begins with the sound they see as they catch the ball.

Vowel Pizza

Skills:
phonemic awareness; understanding vowel sounds

Materials:
• six paper plates
• crayons
• markers

DIRECTIONS:

Decorate each plate with crayons to look like a pepperoni pizza. Print a different vowel sound in the middle of five of the plates. Sing the song below, holding up corresponding "pizzas" as you sing:

Pepperoni Pizza (Tune: "How Dry I Am")
(Children echo back each line.)

> I like to eat
> Pepperoni pizza.
> Pepperoni pizza,
> I like to eat.

2nd Verse - Insert the long "A" sound for every vowel.
> A lake tay ate
> Papparanay pazzay.
> Papparanay pazzay,
> A lake tay ate.

3rd Verse - Insert long *E* sound - "Ee leek tee eat..."

4th Verse - Insert long *I* sound - "I like tie ite..."

5th Verse - Insert long *O* sound - "O loke toe ote..."

6th Verse - Insert long *U* sound - "U luke tuu ute..."

ADAPTATION:

Introduce children to the concept that vowels are letters that can change their sound.

Word Family Rimes

DIRECTIONS:

Make some of the common rimes (word endings) below on the overhead projector with the magnetic letters one at a time. Demonstrate how to create new words by changing the initial consonant sound (onset). Encourage children to think of other words that rhyme and suggest how they should be spelled.

Skills:
blending sounds; reading rhyming words

Materials:
• overhead projector
• magnetic alphabet letters

<u>at</u>	<u>et</u>	<u>it</u>	<u>ot</u>	<u>ut</u>
<u>an</u>	<u>en</u>	<u>in</u>	<u>on</u>	<u>un</u>
<u>ad</u>	<u>ed</u>	<u>id</u>	<u>od</u>	<u>ump</u>
<u>all</u>	<u>ell</u>	<u>ill</u>	<u>op</u>	<u>up</u>
<u>ake</u>	<u>eat</u>	<u>ike</u>	<u>oke</u>	
<u>ay</u>	<u>est</u>	<u>ight</u>	<u>own</u>	
<u>ame</u>	<u>eep</u>	<u>ice</u>		
<u>ain</u>		<u>ing</u>		

ADAPTATIONS:

Let the children use the overhead projector and magnetic letters independently to make words, their names, etc.

Use unit blocks to reinforce word families. Write consonants on 3" squares and tape to smaller blocks. Write word endings on 3" x 6" paper and tape to larger blocks. Change small blocks to make new words.

Rime Associations

Skill:
reading rhyming words

Materials:
• poster board
• scissors
• markers
• crayons

DIRECTIONS:

Cut out shapes from poster board similar to those below. They should each be approximately 9" x 12". Decorate with crayons and cut out a 1½" square in each as shown. Write the rime (word ending) on each cutout. Cut strips from the poster board scraps that are 1½" x 18". Print different consonants on these strips. Cut 3" x 2" pieces of poster board and tape them over the back of the openings to make a guide for the strips. Insert the strips in the guide and slide them up and down to make different words. Read over these words as a group, then encourage children to work with them independently.

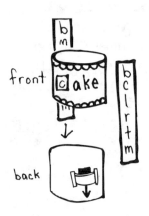

ADAPTATIONS:

To challenge children, write blends and digraphs on strips.

Make rime wheels from two paper plates. Cut a "piece" out of one plate and attach it to the center of the second plate with a brad. Write the rime on the top plate. Write the onsets on the bottom plate so a new word is revealed as you spin it.

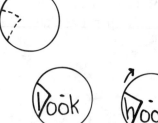

Letter Tiles

DIRECTIONS:

Print a letter on each tile with the permanent marker. (Make duplicates of letters that are frequently used, such as vowels and *l, s, p, t, b,* and *d.*) Demonstrate how to take the letters and put them together to make a word. Make individual letter sounds, then blend the sounds together as you say the word. Change tiles one at a time to create new words.

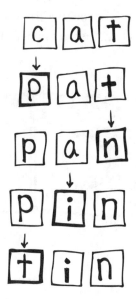

Have children choose tiles and make their names or other words they can read. Store the letter tiles in a small box and add to the writing center.

ADAPTATION:

Pieces from an old Scrabble™ game can also be used for this activity.

*HINT! Check with home building stores or builders to see if they will donate tiles to your classroom for this project.

Skills:
blending sounds; reading simple words

Materials:
- 40 bathroom tiles* (2" in a solid, light color)
- permanent marker (Sharpie™ works well)
- small box

Make Words Book

Skills:
letter/sound
association;
auditory blending

Materials:
- poster board
- tagboard or
  heavy paper
- markers
- binding machine
- $\frac{1}{2}$-inch binder

DIRECTIONS:

Cut two 8½" x 5" sheets of poster board. Cut 20 2½" x 5" rectangles out of heavy paper. On five of the rectangles write one of the following vowels: *a*, *e*, *i*, *o*, and *u*. On ten of the rectangles write one of the following letters: *b*, *c*, *d*, *f*, *p*, *h*, *m*, *s*, *t*, and *r*. On seven of the rectangles write one of the following letters: *p*, *t*, *n*, *d*, *g*, *b*, and *ll*. Lay the five vowels in the middle of one piece of poster board as shown below. Put the set of ten letters on the right, and the set of seven letters on the left. Punch holes and arrange on the binder. Use the second piece of poster board for the cover. Add a title and let the children decorate it. Make new words by flipping different combinations of letters. Say each sound individually as you point to it, then challenge children to blend the sounds together and identify the word.

ADAPTATION:

This game can also be made with heavy cardboard and three book rings. Hole punch the top of each letter and attach to the cardboard with the rings.

SMALL MOTOR SKILLS

EYE-HAND
COORDINATION

MANIPULATIVE
MATERIALS

LEFT-TO-RIGHT
DIRECTIONALITY

PRE-WRITING

PRINTING NAME

WRITING LETTERS

EXPERIMENTING
WITH WRITING

Animal Trails

DIRECTIONS:

Cut out the animals and their homes using the patterns below. Draw a green star on the left side of each sentence strip and glue an animal home to the right side. Make dotted lines as shown from the star on the left to the home on the right. Let the children take the animal cutouts or plastic animals and follow the trail from left to right across the strip.

ant   ant hill

bee   hive

fish   fish bowl

bird   nest

ADAPTATION:

Use play cars, plastic insects, or other small toys to follow paths from left to right. Let children make up their own trails to follow on adding machine tape.

HINT! To help reinforce directionality, give children paper in the shape of pennants for paintings and other art projects.

Small motor

Your Left-Right

DIRECTIONS:

Color the left glove green or write the letter *L* on the back of it with the green marker. Color the right glove red or write the letter *R* on it with the red marker. Put the gloves on your hands and turn your back to the children. Hold up the left glove. Have the children hold up their left hand. Ask them to touch their left ear, left leg, and other body parts on their left side. Do the same thing with the right hand. Explain that whenever you read, you always start at the left and go across to the right side of the page. Demonstrate with a big book or language experience chart. Let the children take turns pointing to where to begin reading and tracking to the right. Ask the children to hold up their left arm. Tie a green piece of yarn around each child's left wrist. Then have them hold up their right arm and tie the red yarn around it. Play "Simon Says" by having the children shake their right arm, stomp their left foot, touch their right ear, etc.

ADAPTATIONS:

Sing the "Hokey Pokey" where the children have to listen to the words and move the appropriate body part. For example:

You put your right arm in, you take your right arm out.

You put your right arm in and you shake it all about.

You do the Hokey Pokey and you turn yourself around.

That's what it's all about!

HINT! Put a little perfume (for girls) or after-shave (for boys) on their wrist to help them remember their "right" hand.

Skill:
left-to-right directionality

Materials:
- gloves (work gloves or old cloth gloves)
- red and green markers
- green yarn and red yarn cut into 12" pieces

Read and Move

Skills:
left-to-right directionality; patterning

Materials:
- large sheets of white paper or tagboard (12"x 24")
- construction paper
- markers
- scissors
- glue
- hole punch
- book rings
- records or tapes with a steady beat

DIRECTIONS:
Cut out the symbols below from construction paper. Use the patterns on the following page.

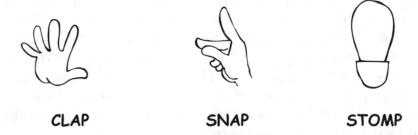

CLAP   SNAP   STOMP

Glue the symbols to the construction paper to represent different patterns (e.g., ABABAB, AABBAABBAABB, etc.). Make the patterns increasingly complex. Have the children "read" the symbols and clap, snap, or stomp accordingly. Play some music and point to the symbols as the children follow along.

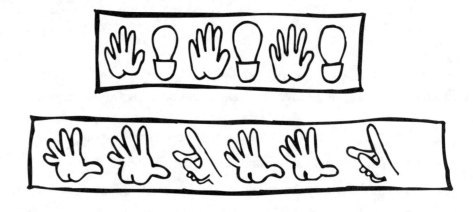

ADAPTATION:
Cut the symbols on the following page out of felt. Let children take turns arranging them in a pattern on a felt board, then have their friends repeat the pattern to music.

Small motor

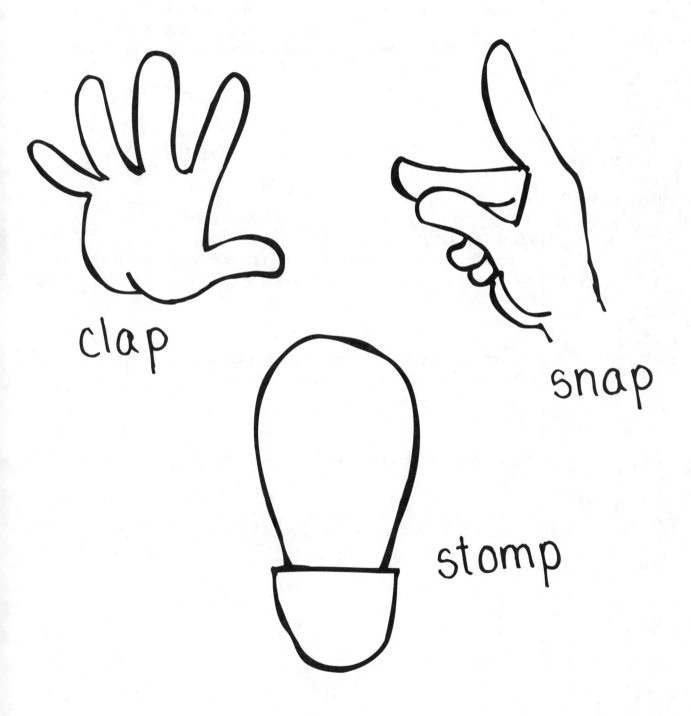

clap

snap

stomp

Magnetic Maze

Skill:
eye-hand coordination

Materials:
- paper plate
- marker
- paper clip
- mouse pattern
- scissors
- small magnet*

DIRECTIONS:
Draw a maze on the paper plate similar to the one below with a magic marker. Cut the mouse out of paper and attach a paper clip to it. Demonstrate how to move the magnet under the paper plate to make the mouse move. Let the children take turns trying to move the mouse through the maze.

ADAPTATIONS:
Draw lines across a cookie sheet with a permanent magic marker. Give the children a small magnetic toy and have them move it from left to right by pulling a magnet underneath.

Let the children draw their own mazes on paper plates, then try to maneuver a paper clip through them with a magnet.

*HINT! Keep magnets away from computers, as they can cause serious damage to them!

string tail

Block Patterns

DIRECTIONS:

Cut square and rectangle shapes from the construction paper using the patterns below. Cut the file folders in half. Arrange the squares and rectangles in different patterns on the file folders. Demonstrate how to look at the patterns and reproduce them with the unit blocks. Place the pattern cards in the block center. Add more difficult patterns as the children's skills improve.

ADAPTATIONS:

Let the children create their own block designs with paper shapes on file folders, then try to reproduce them with real blocks.

Play a game where you hold up a pattern card for several seconds for the child to see. Place it face down on the table, then let him or her try to reproduce it from memory.

Skills:
eye-hand coordination; reproducing a pattern

Materials:
- brown construction paper
- file folders (old ones work well)
- glue
- unit blocks
- scissors

Small motor

Tracking Finger

Skills:
tracking one-to-one; left-to-right directionality

Materials:
- fine tip pen
- big book or language experience chart

DIRECTIONS:

Draw a little face on your index finger similar to the one below. Introduce your finger to the children with this song:

Tracking Finger (Tune: "London Bridge")

Tracking finger says follow me,

Follow me, follow me.

Tracking finger says follow me,

When you want to read.

Demonstrate how to track a line of print as you match the spoken and written word on a big book or chart. Let the children take turns using their "tracking finger" as they read classroom print.

ADAPTATIONS:

Encourage children to use their tracking finger to count on the calendar, read pocket charts, etc.

Use seasonal pencils, chopsticks, or straws as pointers.

Let children make their own "personal pointers" by decorating craft sticks with markers, glitter, and stickers.

Start at the Top

DIRECTIONS:
Teach children this song to sing when they begin to write:

When You Want to Write a Letter
(Tune: "John Brown's Body")

> When you want to write a letter
>
> Start at the top.
>
> When you want to write a letter
>
> Start at the top.
>
> When you want to write a letter
>
> Start at the top
>
> And then you pull down.

ADAPTATIONS:
Model correct writing for children on the chalkboard or large sheets of paper. Point out how you always "start at the top." Ask children other things that always go from the top to the bottom, such as rain, falling leaves, etc.

> Make up songs for writing different letters. For example:
>
> When you want to write a *k*, start at the top.
>
> When you want to write a *k*, start at the top.
>
> Pull straight down, slant in and then out.
>
> When you want to write a *k*, start at the top.

Skills:
pre-writing;
top-to-bottom
orientation

Materials:
• paper
• pencils
• crayons

Small motor

Templates and Tracers

Skills:
pre-writing;
recognizing
shapes

Materials:
• food boxes
  (cut fronts and
  backs off)
  or
• plastic lids
  (take from ice
  cream buckets,
  margarine tubs,
  etc.)
• scissors
• colored pencils
• pens
• paper

DIRECTIONS:

To make stencils, trace shapes on the boxes and lids. Use scissors or a utility knife to cut out the shapes. Give the children colored pencils and paper to trace the shapes.

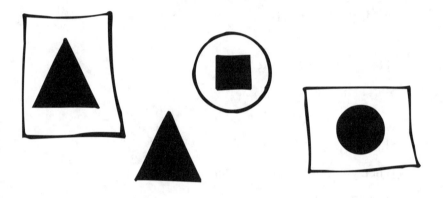

ADAPTATIONS:

Let children color in stencil designs with chalk, crayons, or sponges dipped in paint.

Make letters, numerals, seasonal shapes, or classroom theme stencils.

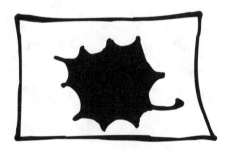

Lines and Curves

DIRECTIONS:

Draw straight or curved lines (similar to the ones below) with markers. Laminate. Give the children play dough and have them roll it out and make lines and curves on the file folders.

Play Dough Recipe

2 C. flour

1 C. salt

2 C. water

*2 TB. Vegetable oil

2 TB. Cream of tartar

food coloring (several drops to desired color)

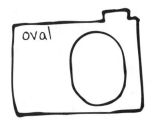

Mix all ingredients together and stir until smooth. Cook over medium heat, stirring constantly. When dough forms a ball and sticks to the spoon, remove from the heat. Knead. Store in a plastic bag.

*Use massage oil in place of the vegetable oil to scent the play dough.

ADAPTATION:

Draw geometric shapes or letters on the file folders for the children to reproduce with the play dough.

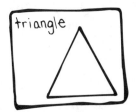

Skill:
pre-writing

Materials:
• old file folders
• markers
• laminating film
• play dough (see recipe at left)

Dot Connection

Skills:
pre-writing;
eye-hand
coordination

Materials:
• clear sheet
  protectors
• white 8½" x 11"
  paper
• markers
• erasable
  markers
• paper towels

DIRECTIONS:

Make different dot configurations (similar to those at right) on the paper with markers. Insert papers in the sheet protectors. Give children vis-à-vis markers with which to connect the dots. Allow them to erase their drawings with a damp paper towel. Ask children to name each shape after they draw it.

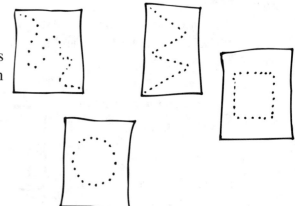

ADAPTATIONS:

Make more complex objects by incorporating one or more shapes.

Make similar dot configurations to help children learn how to make letters, numerals, or write their names.

Add a few drops of food coloring to a bottle of school glue. Shake. Make dots with the colored glue in the shape of letters and words.

HINT! Magnetic sheets from photo albums can also be used.

See and Draw

DIRECTIONS:

Cut file folders in half. Make simple figures and shapes similar to those below on the file folders with markers. Give each child a pencil and a piece of paper. Explain that you will show them a drawing that you want them to look at for a few seconds. Tell them that you will then put the drawing down and let them try to make one just like it on their paper. Begin holding up the first drawing for approximately 15 seconds. Put it face down on the table, then give the children a minute to draw it on their paper. Continue this activity until the children lose interest.

ADAPTATIONS:

Repeat this activity frequently, adding increasingly difficult figures and shapes.

Let children draw objects on the chalkboard or dry erase board, then cover them up while their friends try to draw the same thing.

Skills:
visual memory;
pre-writing;
recognizing
shapes

Materials:
· file folders
· markers
· pencils
· paper

Textured Letters

Skills:
pre-writing;
recognizing
letters

Materials:
- plastic
  needlepoint
  canvas (available
  at craft stores)
  or
- piece of screen
- crayons
- plain white
  paper

DIRECTIONS:

Place a piece of paper on top of the plastic canvas or screen. Write a letter on the paper with a crayon. (This will give the letter a bumpy texture.) Have the child trace over the letter with a finger as he or she reproduces the sound the letter makes.

ADAPTATIONS:

Let the children make their own textured letters using the plastic canvas.

Use this technique to help children learn their names, numerals, sight words, etc.

Children will also enjoy "rub overs." Draw letters or words on poster board with glue. Dry. Have children place a sheet of paper on top, then rub with the side of a crayon. Ask children to identify letters or words from their rubbings.

HINT! Sandpaper or mesh screen can be used in place of plastic canvas.

Sensory Trays

DIRECTIONS:

Cover the bottom of a lunchroom tray or cookie sheet with one of the sensory materials suggested at right. Let the children experiment making drawings and designs. Then have them copy shapes, letters, or their names in the tray.

ADAPTATIONS:

The top of a shirt box, a plastic lid from a deli tray, a cookie sheet, or a stove burner cover can be used in place of the lunchroom tray.

Line the bottom of the container with aluminum foil or colored construction paper for more contrast.

Post copies of shapes or letters near this activity for children to copy.

Fill a heavy-duty zipper bag with one-half cup hair gel. Tape it with duct tape around the edges to a table. Children can trace shapes and designs in the squishy bag.

*HINT! To make rainbow rice, divide a large bag of rice into four small plastic bags. Add one teaspoon of rubbing alcohol and a squirt of food coloring to each bag. Shake. Dry on wax paper. Mix all four colors together.

Materials:
- plastic lunchroom trays or cookie sheets
- sensory materials: sand, rainbow rice*, cornmeal, shaving cream, whipped topping, etc.

Small motor

Sew and Sew

Skill:
eye-hand coordination

Materials:
- cardboard food boxes
- hole punch
- yarn
- pipe cleaner

Materials:
- cardboard scraps
- scissors
- yarn

Materials:
- waxed dental floss
- cereal or pasta with holes

Materials:
- cardboard food boxes
- scissors
- zip baggies

MAKE SMALL MOTOR ACTIVITIES SIMILAR TO THE ONES BELOW FOR CHILDREN TO USE.

Sewing Card
DIRECTIONS:
Cut the fronts off the food boxes. Punch holes around the edges. Cut a pipe cleaner in half, then twist it around the yarn to make a needle. Let children sew around the edges.

ADAPTATIONS:
Cut large letter stencils out of cardboard. Hole punch, then let children lace with yarn or old shoelaces.

Have children sew on burlap with yarn and plastic needles.

Yarn Weaving
DIRECTIONS:
Cut cardboard into geometric shapes, then cut notches along the edges as shown. Children weave yarn through the notches to create designs.

Box Top Puzzles
DIRECTIONS:
Cut the front side off the food boxes. Cut each front into five to ten puzzle shapes; Store in zip baggies.

Stringing Things
DIRECTIONS:
Have children string cereal or pasta on dental floss to make necklaces.

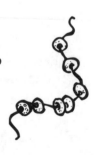

Cut Ups

DIRECTIONS:

Follow the exercises below to help children develop cutting skills.

1st- Give children paper to tear into little pieces with their fingers.

2nd- Allow children to snip the ends of paper with scissors. Remind them to keep their thumb on top.

3rd- Demonstrate how to cut on straight lines to make paper strips.

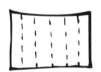

4th- Draw curved lines on paper for children to cut. Show them how to turn the paper as they cut.

5th- Give children simple geometric shapes to cut out.

6th- Let children experiment cutting out wallpaper books, wrapping paper, and magazine pictures.

7th- Have children draw their own shapes and pictures and cut them out.

HINT! Recycle paper-cutting projects by using them to make collages, or stuff cardboard boxes to make blocks.

Skill:
cutting

Materials:
- paper (newsprint, construction paper scraps, wallpaper books, magazines, grocery sacks, wrapping paper, old greeting cards, etc.)
- safety scissors

Story Strokes

Materials:
- large sheets of paper
- crayons or pencils
- chalkboard or dry erase board

DIRECTIONS:

Tell the children that you have a story for them about going to the park. It's a special story because they get to draw it on their paper as you tell it. Give each child a large sheet of paper and a crayon or pencil. Have them make a little mark on the left hand side of their paper so they will know where to begin. Demonstrate the story strokes below on a chalkboard or dry erase board as you tell it to the children.

A Walk in the Park

One day I went for a walk in the park.

I saw some clouds rolling in the sky.

I saw birds flying from tree to tree.

I saw ducks swimming in the pond.

Some children were swinging.

A little rabbit hopped up and down.

Then it started to rain hard.

So I ran home as fast as I could!

ADAPTATIONS:

Make up other stories that relate to seasonal events and incorporate similar writing strokes.

Let children make up their own stories and strokes and demonstrate them on the board.

Invisible Writing

DIRECTIONS:

Ask the children if they know what "invisible writing" is. Demonstrate invisible writing by holding your finger in the air and making a letter. (Turn your back to the children as you do this so they will see the proper formation. Otherwise, they will see it backwards!) Have the children follow along as you make different letters in the air. Describe the strokes as you make them. For example: "Let's make a *p*. First, you make a circle, then you pull down. Now you do it with me." After you make each letter, remind the children to "erase" it by taking the palm of their hand and moving it in a circular motion!

ADAPTATIONS:

Give the children a wet sponge and have them write different letters on the chalkboard. Why do they disappear?

On the playground, give children a paintbrush and a bucket of water with which to paint letters on the sidewalk or building.

Give children a flashlight and have them make letters on the wall or ceiling. They will also enjoy tracking a line of print with a flashlight in a big book or on a language experience chart.

Write letters on the children's backs, or let them take turns writing letters on each other's backs. Trace letters on the palm of children's hands.

 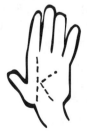

Wiggly Worms

Skills:
eye-hand coordination; pre-writing

Materials:
- 18" piece of colorful yarn for each child

DIRECTIONS:

Give each child a piece of yarn and explain that it is a wiggly worm. Have them wiggle it on their head, chin, back, knee, and on other parts of their body. After several minutes of free exploration, ask the children to place their worms on the floor. Can they make something with their worm? Can they make a shape with it? Can they make a letter? Can they make the letter that their name starts with? Point to different letters around the room or call out different letters for the children to reproduce with their piece of yarn.

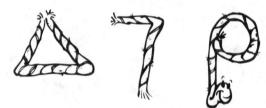

ADAPTATIONS:

Play a game where children make letters with their yarn, then their classmates try to identify what they are.

Demonstrate how to form different letters by using a piece of yarn on a flannel board. Ask the children to copy what you do.

Use Wikki Stix™, pipe cleaners, wire, clay, and other materials to make letters.

Let children glue yarn to paper to write initials, names, and words.

Small motor

Rainbow Names

DIRECTIONS:

Print each child's name on a piece of paper. Demonstrate how to take different colors and go around each letter. Let the children trace around the letters in their name to make a rainbow.

ADAPTATIONS:

Have children trace around other words they want to learn with different colors of crayons.

Let children write their names with glue, then sprinkle over with glitter.

Use sand, colored rice, yarn, beans, and other sensory materials to make children's names.

Give children chalk to practice writing their names on the sidewalk.

Have children trace over their names with tracing paper or clear overhead projector sheets.

Make "scratch and sniff" name cards. Write children's names with glue on poster board. Sprinkle with flavored gelatin mix. Dry. Children can trace and "sniff" their letters.

HINT! As children master writing their first name, encourage them to write their last name.

Sign In, Please

DIRECTIONS:

Write "Sign In, Please" at the top of the poster board. Laminate it or cover with clear contact paper. Tape the poster on your classroom door and attach a vis-à-vis marker with a string. As each child arrives, he or she can write their name or "make their mark." At group time, count the number of signatures each day and then count the children present. Check to see who "forgot" to sign in. Stress the importance of writing their name to let you know they are at school. (Choose one child to erase the names with a wet towel at the end of each day.)

ADAPTATIONS:

Have the children write their first and last names or their initials, or draw their face on the poster.

Use a clipboard to make a waiting list so children can sign up to play in a center, use the computer, or read with the teacher at independent reading time.

Make a large class roster on a language experience chart. Have one child be teacher and "call roll" each day and check off the friends who are present. Show them how to make a "✔" if children are present, and an "X" if they are absent.

Who's here?			
Gail	✓	✓	✓
Lee	✓	X	✓
Wade	X	X	✓
Jim	✓	✓	✓

Small motor

Writing Slate

DIRECTIONS:

Stuff the empty cereal boxes with newspaper and tape shut. Cover each box with white contact paper. Give the children erasable markers to write or draw pictures on their slates. They can easily clean them with a damp towel or sponge.

ADAPTATIONS:

Make a slate for each child. Write their name on it in permanent marker so they can use it for a model as they practice writing their names.

Store the boxes on a shelf side-by-side like books.

Use the slates with older children. Have them write letters, shapes, words, etc.

Cover a large corrugated cardboard box with the white contact paper so several children at a time can draw and write.

Purchase a large piece of dry erase board at a hardware store or lumberyard. Have them cut it into smaller sections (approximately 16" x 18"). Store in a plastic crate for children to use independently. (You must use dry erase markers with these. Use an old sock for an eraser.)

HINT! Children can also write on pages from a magnetic photo album with water-soluble markers.

Skill:
writing

Materials:
- empty cereal boxes
- newspaper
- tape
- white contact paper
- water-soluble markers
- damp paper towel or sponge

E-Mail

Skill:
interest in print (using computer terminology)

Materials:
- cereal box or shoebox to make a mailbox or computer
- pens
- pencils
- crayons
- rubber stamps etc.

DIRECTIONS:

Cut off the top of the box, then cover it with paper. Cut a flag out of cardboard and attach it to the side of the box with the brad. Write "E-Mail" on the box. Cut out self-closing envelopes using the pattern below. Place the mailbox and envelopes in your writing center or on a small table.

Post a class roster so the children will know how to spell each other's names. Demonstrate how to write a note, then fold the envelope, put a friend's name on the front, and mail it in the box. Choose different children to deliver messages at the end of the day.

Ask children if they know what e-mail is. Explain that it stands for "electronic mail," but your e-mail will stand for "easy mail."

Pattern for self-closing envelope

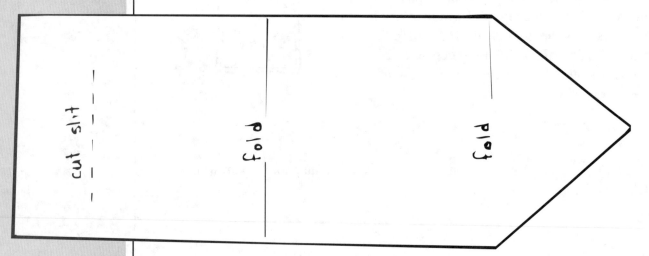

Secret Spelling

DIRECTIONS:

Guide children in beginning writing by using this strategy.

Stage one: Have them clap out the number of words they want to say. Tell them to make a line on their paper for each word. (Explain that it's "secret spelling" because nobody knows what it says but them!) The teacher then writes the words on the lines as the child dictates them. Read over the words together.

Stage two: After the children make lines on their page for the words they want to say, encourage them to go back and write the letters that they hear at the beginning of each word.

Stage three: As the children progress, challenge them to write final sounds they hear in each word.

Stage four: Children can begin to include other sounds they hear.

Materials:
- paper
- pencils
- pens

Journals

Skills:
writing; reading

Materials:
- construction paper (12" x 18")
- hole punch
- yarn
- paper (8½" x 11")
- markers
- crayons
- art supplies

DIRECTIONS:
Let children make journals at the beginning of each month. First, let them look at a calendar to determine how many days they will be in school. Then let them count out the number of sheets of paper they will need. Have them put the paper inside a sheet of construction paper to make a book. Punch two holes on the top or side (depending on the direction you want the book to open). Tie with yarn. Let the children decorate their covers with markers, crayons, and other art supplies. Set aside a time each day for the children to write or draw in their journals. (Be available to take dictation for younger children.)

ADAPTATIONS:
Give children the opportunity to read their journals aloud to classmates.

Have the teacher or parents write comments to the children in their journals.

Focus journal writing on friendships, current projects, literature read, or other themes.

Write responses back to children in their journals.

Save the journals through the year and give them to the parents at your end-of-year conference.

Use journals to assess children's reading and writing skills.

Use wallpaper, fabric scraps, contact paper, and other materials to make covers for journals.

HINT! Model journal writing by doing it as a large-group activity on the board at the beginning of the year. After doing this together for several weeks, children may feel more confident about writing independently.

Personal Stationery

DIRECTIONS:

Glue each child's photograph on the corner of a piece of paper. Run off 10–20 copies of each sheet. Write each child's name on a file folder and file the papers with their picture in their respective folder. Store the folders in a plastic crate. Tell the children that you've made a surprise for each of them—it's their own personal stationery! Whenever they want to write a letter, draw a picture, or write a story, they can get a piece of their own stationery. Show children the folders and how to find their name and stationery. Place the crate in the writing center.

ADAPTATIONS:

Let children use their stationery when you make class books.

Have children design borders around their stationery or write their names before you copy them.

Use photograph stationery to send home personal notes to parents.

HINT! Use lined or unlined paper, depending on the skill level of the students in your class.

Skill:
writing

Materials:
- individual photographs of children
- glue
- paper
- copy machine
- file folders
- plastic basket
- pens
- pencils
- crayons

Punctuation Spotter

Skill:
identifying punctuation

Materials:
plastic fly swatter, language experience charts, big books

DIRECTIONS:

Cut a 1½" square from the middle of the fly swatter. Explain that when you drive a car there are different signs to tell you what to do. For example, a red light means you stop, a green light means you go, and a yellow light means slow down. When you write and read, there are also signs to follow. Show the children the fly swatter. Explain that it's a "punctuation spotter," which will help them learn signs for reading and writing. Isolate a period on a language experience chart. Ask the children if they know what it is called. Explain that a period is like a stop sign that tells them to stop because it is the end of the sentence. A new sentence will always begin with a capital letter. Next, highlight a question mark, then an exclamation point. Demonstrate how punctuation can change the meaning of a sentence by reading the sentences below:

My dog is lost.

My dog is lost?

My dog is lost!

Have the children take the punctuation spotter and identify other periods, question marks, and exclamation points on classroom print.

ADAPTATIONS:

Introduce commas and quotation marks.

Always point out punctuation marks as you model writing for children. When they dictate a sentence to you, ask them what punctuation mark belongs at the end.

Alphabet Art

DIRECTIONS:

Coordinate art projects with letters children are learning. Some suggestions are:

A- APPLE PRINTS   N- NEWSPAPER COLLAGE

B- BUBBLE PRINTS   O- ORANGE PRINTS

C- COTTON COLLAGE   P- POTATO PRINTS

D- DIRT PAINTING   Q- Q-TIP PAINTING

E- ELBOW PAINTING   R- RUBBINGS

F- FEATHER PAINTING   S- SPONGE ART

G- GLUE PAINTING   T- TOOTHPICK COLLAGE

H- HAND PRINTS   U- UPSIDE DOWN PICTURE

I- ICE CUBE PAINTING   V- VEGETABLE PRINTS

J- JELLY PAINTING   W- WALLPAPER COLLAGE

K- KITE SHAPES   X- "X" MARKS THE SPOT

L- LEAF COLLAGE   Y- YARN COLLAGE

M- MARBLE PAINTING   Z- ZOOM! RACE CAR PAINTING

ADAPTATIONS:

File these projects after the children complete them. Then put them together at the end of the school year to make an "Alphabet Art Book."

Give each child an 8" paper square. Assign each a different letter to write on his or her square. Have them draw an object that begins with that sound. Hole punch the corners of each square and tie together to make an alphabet quilt.

Small motor

Artsy Ideas

Enhance letter recognition with one of these activities:

Sponge Prints

DIRECTIONS:

Cut sponges into letter shapes. Let children sponge paint designs on paper or spell out words with the sponges.

Giant Letters

DIRECTIONS:

Draw giant letters on the poster board and cut them out. Have children cut out magazine pictures of objects that begin with that sound and glue them on the poster. Children could also make a collage on the letter with materials that start with that sound. For example, ribbon could be glued on the *r* or noodles on the *n*.

Letter Collage

DIRECTIONS:

Draw letters with glue on heavy paper, then glue one of the items listed at left on top. (Try to use objects that begin with the letter sound. For example, beans for *b*, feathers for *f*, toothpicks for *t*, etc.)

Spaghetti Art

DIRECTIONS:

Arrange cooked spaghetti noodles on a piece of paper in the shape of letters or words. As they dry, they will stick to the paper.

Materials:
- cooked spaghetti noodles
- paper

3-D Art

DIRECTIONS:

Let children make three-dimensional letters with the materials above.

Materials:
- clay
- aluminum foil
- pipe cleaners
- wood scraps

Textured Paint

DIRECTIONS:

Mix equal parts of flour and salt. Stir together. Encourage children to paint letters and shapes with a paintbrush or Q-Tip™.

Materials:
- flour
- salt
- liquid tempera
- paper
- brushes

Easel Letters

DIRECTIONS:

Ask children to paint letters at the easel with various media. Have them paint objects that begin with a sound you are working on.

Materials:
- art easel
- large paper
- paint
- paintbrushes
- water colors
- chalk
- markers
- crayons

Edible Letters

USE ONE OF THE ACTIVITIES BELOW TO REINFORCE LETTER RECOGNITION.

Pretzel Nibbles

DIRECTIONS:

Give children several pretzel twists and sticks. Show them how to nibble the twists and put them with the sticks to form different letters. Let them experiment by making letters and eating them.

ADAPTATION:

Pair children and let them take turns making letters while their friend tries to guess what letter it is. Have children write their names or simple words with pretzels.

Cheesy Letters

DIRECTIONS:

Let children squirt cheese on crackers in the shape of letters. Demonstrate how to lick the letter off as you reproduce the sound it makes.

ADAPTATION:

A sweet version of this can be done with squirt icing on graham crackers.

Letter Bread

DIRECTIONS:

Fill each cup half full with milk. Color the milk with food coloring. Give children Q-Tips™ with which to paint letters on their bread with the colored milk. Toast.

Bread Dough Letters

DIRECTIONS:

Thaw bread dough. Have children wash their hands, then give each of them a ball of dough on a piece of wax paper. Have children rub a little oil on their hands and roll and mold the dough into a letter. Bake on a greased cookie sheet at 350° until lightly browned.

ADAPTATION:

Give children packaged cookie dough to form into letters. Bake and eat.

Chocolate Letters

DIRECTIONS:

Prepare dough by mixing the peanut butter, icing, and dry milk. Give each child a spoonful on a piece of wax paper. Let them make letters or objects that begin with a sound you are working on.

Materials:
- frozen bread dough
- wax paper
- cooking sheet
- vegetable oil

Materials:
- 1 cup smooth peanut butter
- 1 cup canned chocolate icing
- 1½ cups instant nonfat dry milk
- wax paper

Outdoor Fun

Skill:
recognizing letters
and words

Materials:
• paint brushes
• buckets of water

Materials:
• colored plastic
  cups
• chain link fence

Materials:
• sandbox

Materials:
• colored chalk
• sidewalk

Here are some fun ways to integrate literacy with outdoor play.

Water Painting
DIRECTIONS:

Let children experiment by painting with the water on trees, playground equipment, and the sidewalk. Ask them to paint shapes, letters, their names, or words.

Fence Designs
DIRECTIONS:

Insert cups in the fence to make designs, letters, and words.

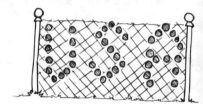

Sand Writing
DIRECTIONS:

Demonstrate how to smooth out the sand, then draw shapes, letters, and words. (You may use your finger or a stick.)

Hopscotch
DIRECTIONS:

Draw a hopscotch board on the sidewalk. Put letters in each section. Children hop on the board and name each letter as they step on it.

ADAPTATION:

Make letter hopscotch in the classroom with colored tape.

Follow the Line
DIRECTIONS:

Draw giant letters on the sidewalk with chalk. Have children walk, tiptoe, jump, bounce a ball, or ride a tricycle along the line.

ORAL LANGUAGE SKILLS

COMMUNICATION

VOCABULARY

CONNECTION BETWEEN SPOKEN AND PRINTED WORD

CONCEPT DEVELOPMENT

CONTEXT CLUES

STORYTELLING

DRAMATIZATIONS

Talking Wand

Skill:
oral language

Materials:
- 12"-16" wooden stick or cardboard roller from a pants hanger
- aluminum foil
- glue
- glitter

DIRECTIONS:
Make a "talking wand" by covering the stick or cardboard roller with aluminum foil. Dip the end in glue, then roll in glitter. Have the children sit in a circle. Show the children the "magic talking wand." Explain that whoever is holding it may have a turn talking. Everyone else must listen. Pass the stick around for each child to have a turn.

ADAPTATIONS:
Tape-record the children talking, then play it back for them.

Use the talking wand at the end of the day for recall. Let each child hold it and tell one new thing he or she learned.

Start a sentence, then pass the wand around the group as each child completes it. For example, "If I were an animal, I would like to be a/an _____"; "When I get angry I _____"; " I wish I were_____ years old because _____."

Tell Me a Story

DIRECTIONS:

Decorate the outside of the canister with construction paper and simple drawings. Cut the paper in 10" x 2½" strips. Place a different sticker or picture at the bottom of each strip. Put the strips in the canister with the pictures on the bottom. Have the children sit in a circle. Pass the canister around and ask each child to pull out a strip. Let them make up a sentence or a story about the picture on the bottom of their strip.

ADAPTATIONS:

Put interesting objects in a small box (toys, objects from nature, "junk," etc.). Children choose an object, draw a picture of it, then make up a story about it.

Hide small objects or pictures in lunch sacks. Divide children into groups and give each group a lunch sack. Have each child make up a different story about the object or picture in the bag.

Materials:
- potato chip canister
- heavy paper
- scissors
- stickers or small pictures
- glue
- construction paper
- markers

Language Experience Charts

Skill:
making connections between spoken word and print

Materials:
- large chart paper (lined)
- markers
- chart easel

DIRECTIONS:

Use language experience charts to record children's speech, then read back over what they have dictated.

Field Trips: Have children recall experiences from a field trip in sequential order.

Class Parties: Let each child dictate what he or she liked best about a class party or special event.

Super Star: Choose one child each week to be the "super star." Write his or her name at the top of the chart, then ask each classmate to dictate what they like best about that person.

KWL: When starting a new unit or topic of study, ask children what they **K**now about the topic and what they **W**ant to learn about the topic. As they **L**earn new information, add it to the chart.

Story Recall: Have children recall the events of the story in sequential order as you write them on the chart.

Daily News: At the conclusion of each day, have children recall the day as you write their comments.

Complete the Sentence: Write part of a sentence at the top of the chart, then write children's names and how they would complete the sentence.
For example: "I am special because _____";
    "When I grow up I want to be a/an _____";
    "I like to read _____";
    "My favorite center at school is _____".

Brainstorm: Involve children in brainstorming all the uses of an object (such as a rubber band); ways to solve a problem (e.g., not putting away toys at school); or things you can learn from a book!

HINT! Attach two book rings to a hanger. Language experience charts can be attached to the book rings and hung any place in the room. (Skirt hangers can also be used.)

Cut-Apart Chart

DIRECTIONS:

Begin a language experience story with the children about a familiar topic, such as food, animals, a holiday, field trip, etc. Write the title of the story at the top of the chart. Guide children in dictating sentences so the vocabulary is fairly repetitive. Have children read over the sentences with you. Write duplicates of each sentence on a sentence strip. Pass out the sentences, then have the children match up their sentence with the matching sentence on the chart. Next, cut apart each sentence strip between the words. Put the pieces for each sentence in a different baggie. Pass out the baggies to the children. Have them "shake" up their bags, then put their sentences together and read them.

Ask children to count the number of words in their sentence. What kind of letter does their sentence begin with? What is at the end?

Birds

Birds can fly.
Birds have feathers.
Birds have beaks.
Birds build nests.
We like birds.

Birds have feathers.

Birds | have | beaks.

We | like | birds.

ADAPTATIONS:

Use a pocket chart for this activity.

Take familiar songs, nursery rhymes, chants, or poems and write them on a language experience chart. Make duplicates of each line for the children to match up, then cut apart to make sentence puzzles.

Materials:
- language experience chart
- sentence strips
- markers
- scissors
- zipper bags

Oral language

Picture Talks

Skills:
building vocabulary; making connections between spoken word and print

Materials:
- magazine pictures
- large sheets of newsprint
- scissors
- glue
- markers

DIRECTIONS:

Cut out an interesting magazine picture and glue it to the middle of the paper. Ask the children to look at the picture and think of words that describe it. As each child says a word, write it on the paper and make a line connecting it to the appropriate detail in the picture. Summarize the activity by reading over the words together.

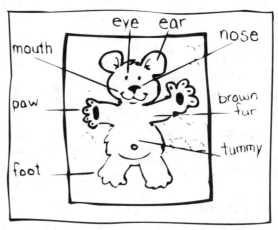

ADAPTATIONS:

Use pictures from newspapers to increase children's awareness of current events.

Use book covers to make picture maps about what children think the story will be about.

HINT! Tie in picture talks with classroom themes or topics that children are interested in.

Fill In the Blank

DIRECTIONS:

Tell stories similar to the one below and let the children supply a missing word whenever you come to a blank.

One day Old MacDonald woke up and went out to the _____.

He saw _____ and _____ and _____. He fed the cows _____. Then he fed the chickens_____, and finally he fed the pigs _____. The farmer got on his _____ and drove out to his fields. He planted _____ and _____.

He was very hungry from working so hard, so he went home and ate_____. Then he lay down and went to _____.

ADAPTATIONS:

Make up other imaginary stories with toys and puppets. For example, hold up a stuffed animal as you tell the story below:

> This is _____.
>
> It likes to eat _____.
>
> Its favorite book to read is _____.
>
> When boys and girls leave in the afternoon it _____.

As you read books to children, stop occasionally and let them guess the next word.

Put a book down before you get to the end and let the children make up their own endings.

Have children supply missing words as you sing songs, do finger plays, or say rhymes.

Skills:
supplying missing words; using context clues

Materials:
none

Tunes for Addresses and Phone Numbers

Skill:
repeating
personal
information

Materials:
• list of
children's
addresses and
phone numbers

DIRECTIONS:

Sing each child's address to the tune of "Do You Know the Muffin Man?"

For example: 495 Jersey Lane, Jersey Lane, Jersey Lane.

495 Jersey Lane is where Mishka lives.

Sing each child's phone number to the tune of "Twinkle, Twinkle, Little Star."

For example: 3 8 1 - 4 6 2 2, 3 8 1 - 4 6 2 2.

3 8 1 - 4 6 2 2, I can say my phone for you.

3 8 1 - 4 6 2 2, 3 8 1 - 4 6 2 2.

Teach your city or town and Zip code to the tune of "Bingo."

For example: There is a city that we love,

Atlanta is its name-o

30345, 30345, 30345,

And that is the Zip code.

ADAPTATIONS:

Children can learn their birthday to the tune of "Happy Birthday to You."

For example: July 15th, July 15th,

My special birthday is

July 15th.

HINT! Talk about why it is important for children to know their phone numbers and addresses. How would this help them in an emergency?

Busy Bee

DIRECTIONS:

Make a bee for each child using the pattern on the bottom of the page. (Older children can color and cut out their own bees.) Tape bees to the ends of straws. Have children take their bees and follow directions as you say the poem below.

Busy Bees

Busy bees, busy bees, flying all around.

Busy bees up, and busy bees down.

Busy bees fly with a buzzing sound.

Buzzzz! On your ear.

Buzzzz! Above your head.

Buzzzz! Under your leg.

Buzzzz! Behind your back.

Continue naming different body parts and prepositions (over, beneath, between, beside, in front of, etc.) where children can place their bees.

ADAPTATIONS:

For younger children, demonstrate positions and have them follow along.

Let children call out directions for where bees should "buzz."

Take a small toy and move it around the room (e.g., on a child's head, under a table, next to the door, etc.). Have children describe where the toy is as it changes positions.

Skills:
demonstrating positional prepositions; following directions

Materials:
- copy of bee for each child
- straw
- tape
- scissors
- crayons

The Opposite Song

Skill:
demonstrating opposites

Materials:
none

DIRECTIONS:

Sing the song below and have the children follow the motions that you do.

The Opposite Song (Tune: "Shortnin' Bread")

We can do opposites, opposites, opposites.	(Clap hands)
We can do opposites, look and see.	
Top and bottom, top and bottom,	(Touch top of head,
Top and bottom, just like me.	then bottom of foot)
Front and back, front and back,	(Touch tummy, then
Front and back, just like me.	back)

Continue singing and acting out different opposites, such as "right and left," "in and out," "happy and sad," "over and under," etc.

ADAPTATIONS:

Have the children suggest other opposites you can sing and act out.

Make a book of opposites. Have each child fold a piece of paper in half and draw a line down the middle. Ask them to draw pictures of opposites on each side and label.

Concept Toss

DIRECTIONS:

Entertain children and reinforce skills as you line them up or change activities with this game. Take the beanbag or ball and name a category. Tell the children that when you toss them the beanbag they must name an object in that category as they catch it. Categories might include: foods, places, things that are yellow, objects that begin with the letter *g*, etc.

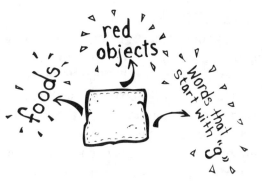

ADAPTATIONS:

Let the children take turns naming categories and tossing the beanbag to a friend.

Make a list of all the objects children can name in a given category.

Play a similar rhyming game with a ball. Have children sit in a circle. Say a word, then roll the ball to a child. That child must catch the ball and think of a word that rhymes with the one you said.

Skill:
naming objects in a given category

Materials:
· beanbag or small sponge ball

Story Headbands

DIRECTIONS:

Cut out felt pieces using the patterns on page 162. Glue these to the headbands to make props for the children to wear. Read the story "Room for One More!" (page 161). To begin, sit in a chair and hold a closed umbrella. Each time a character joins the story, push the umbrella up a little. When the bear arrives on the scene, the umbrella should be fully opened. When the ant squeezes in, quickly close the umbrella with a "POP!" Pass out headbands to the children. Tell them to come up and join you as their name is mentioned in the story. Encourage them to ask if they may come under the umbrella and to remember to use the words "please" and "thank you."

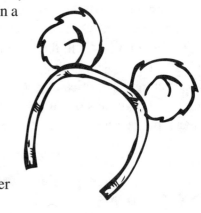

ADAPTATIONS:

After acting out the story, have the children recall the order in which the animals joined in. Act out the story many times so that all children have the opportunity to play a part. Place the headbands in the dramatic play area to encourage further role playing and experimentation with language.

Make story headbands for "Goldilocks and the Three Bears," "The Three Billy Goats Gruff," "The Three Little Pigs," "The Little Red Hen," and other favorite tales.

Room for One More!

Once there was a little mouse who lived in the forest. One day it started to rain, so he ran and hid under a mushroom. It was just the right size for a little mouse—a perfect umbrella.

Soon a frog hopped by. "Say, may I please join you?" asked the frog politely.

"I suppose there's always room for one more," answered the mouse.

So the mouse moved over and made room for the frog, and the mushroom grew a little.

Along came a little bird. "Please, do you think you could let me in under the mushroom? I'm getting awfully wet out here," said the little bird.

"Well, we'll squeeze in a little. There's always room for one more," replied the mouse. The mushroom grew a little more.

It wasn't long before a little squirrel came scampering by. "Please, may I come in with you? I do hate to get my bushy tail wet," asked the squirrel.

"There's always room for one more," answered the mouse as the mushroom grew even bigger.

Along hopped a little rabbit. The other animals looked so cozy huddled together under the mushroom that the rabbit asked, "May I join you, please?"

"There's always room for one more," answered the mouse as the mushroom grew even bigger.

Next a fox came by. "I'm so wet and cold," said the fox. "May I please join you under the mushroom?"

"Always room for one more," said the mouse as the other animals squeezed in tighter. The mushroom grew just a little bigger.

Finally a big bear came along. "Please, please, may I come in out of the rain with you?" begged the bear.

"Oh, dear," thought the mouse. "Well, there's always room for one more, I guess."

The animals huddled in closer and the mushroom grew as big as it could.

Just then a little ant crawled by. Without so much as a "please" or "thank you," that little ant tried to join the others under the mushroom. That little ant just pushed and shoved until POP! The mushroom burst into a million pieces. And what do you think happened then? That's right! All the animals had to scurry and find another place to keep dry. (Children run and hide around the room.)

STORY HEADBAND CUTOUTS

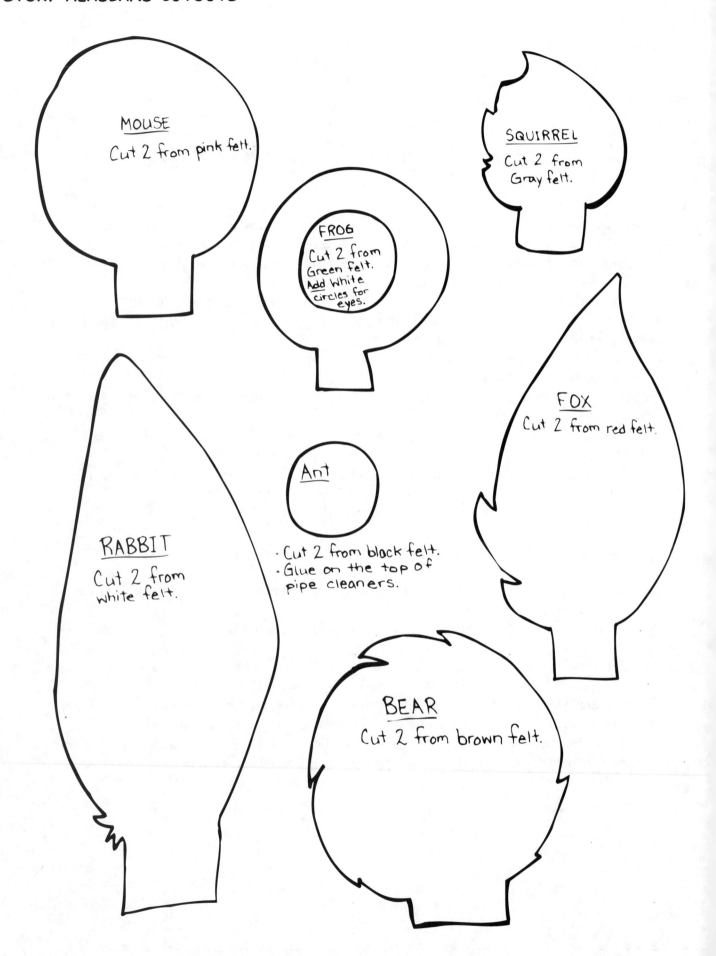

MOUSE
Cut 2 from pink felt.

SQUIRREL
Cut 2 from Gray felt.

FROG
Cut 2 from Green felt. Add White circles for eyes.

FOX
Cut 2 from red felt.

Ant
· Cut 2 from black felt.
· Glue on the top of pipe cleaners.

RABBIT
Cut 2 from white felt.

BEAR
Cut 2 from brown felt.

Story House

DIRECTIONS:

Staple up the bottom flap on the sack in the back to create a pocket. Fold down the top corners toward the back to create a triangle. Tape in place. Turn the sack over; it should look like a house. Let the children decorate their houses with crayons or markers. Have them look through the magazines or catalogs and find people to live in their house. Tape these to Popsicle™ sticks in order to make puppets. Children can make up stories with their puppets, then store them in the pocket in the back of their house.

Skill:
retelling a story

Materials:
- large paper grocery sacks
- scissors
- markers
- crayons
- tape
- stapler
- magazines
- catalogs
- Popsicle™ sticks

FRONT   BACK

ADAPTATIONS:

Have children draw family members on heavy paper, cut them out, and tape them to Popsicle sticks.

Make a story house for retelling "Little Red Riding Hood." Color and cut out the characters on the following page. Tape them to Popsicle sticks and store them in the back of the sack house.

Let children make story houses and puppets for "The Gingerbread Man," "The Three Bears," "Hansel and Gretel," "The Three Little Pigs," and other fairy tales.

"LITTLE RED RIDING HOOD" STICK PUPPETS
Color, cut out, and tape to Popsicle sticks.

Little Red Riding Hood

Wolf

Grandmother

Wolf dressed as Grandmother

Overhead Projector Story

DIRECTIONS:

Cut out the story pieces for the three billy goats and the troll on the following page. Tape these to straws. Cut out the bridge and place it on the bottom of the overhead projector. Move the pieces to the overhead projector as you retell the story of "The Three Billy Goats Gruff."

ADAPTATIONS:

Let children retell the story with the puppets on the overhead.

Read several different versions of "The Three Billy Goats Gruff" and compare.

Have children make their own shadow puppets by cutting characters and props out of paper and taping them to straws.

Give children clear overhead projector sheets and markers to illustrate stories. Project these on the wall, encouraging children to describe their pictures.

Skill:
retelling a story in sequence

Materials:
- copy of story pieces on the following page
- scissors
- tape
- straw
- overhead projector

SHADOW PUPPETS FOR "THE THREE BILLY GOATS GRUFF"

Story Box

DIRECTIONS:

Cut a piece of felt the size of the box and glue it to the inside cover. Cut the felt pieces for the story of "The Three Little Pigs" using the patterns on the following page. Decorate with wiggly eyes and felt pieces. Demonstrate how to tell the story with the pieces on the felt board in the box. Place the pieces inside, then put the box in your classroom library so the children can practice retelling it to each other.

ADAPTATIONS:

Allow the children to take the story box home and share it with their families.

Make story boxes for other folk tales, such as "The Gingerbread Boy," "Little Red Riding Hood," "The Three Bears," "The Little Red Hen," and other favorites.

Skill:
retelling a story

Materials:
- cigar box, pizza box, or other medium-size box with a lid attached
- felt
- felt scraps
- wiggly eyes
- scissors
- fabric glue

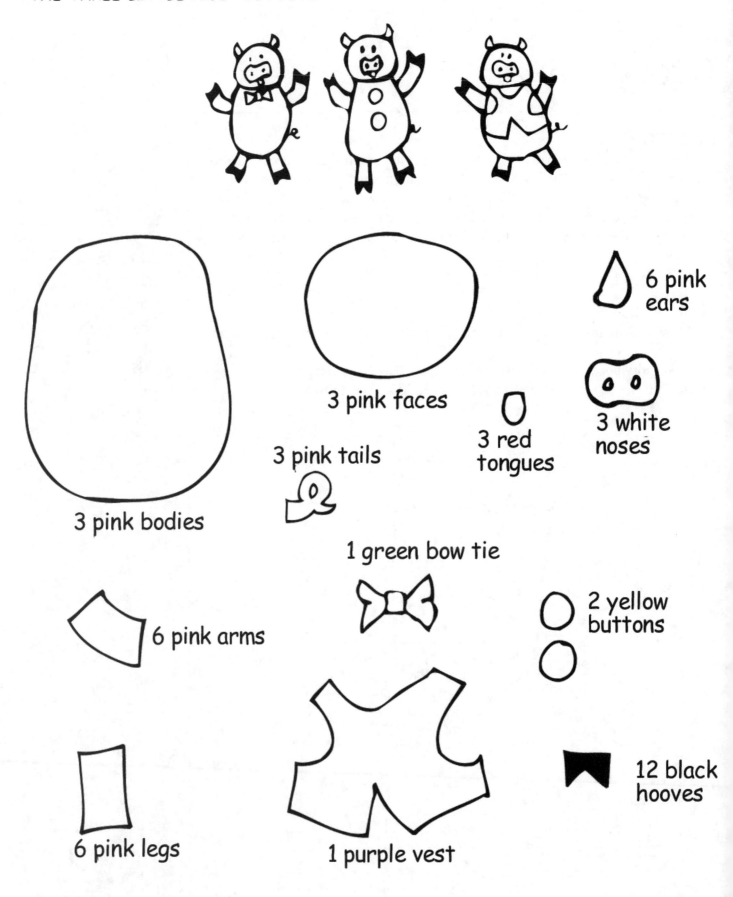

3 pink bodies

3 pink faces

3 pink tails

6 pink ears

3 red tongues

3 white noses

6 pink arms

1 green bow tie

2 yellow buttons

6 pink legs

1 purple vest

12 black hooves

I gray arm

O black nose

O red tongue

I gray tail

1 gray wolf

Cut 3 houses

l yellow (straw)
l brown (stick)
l red (brick)

Story Apron

Skill:
retelling a story
in sequence

Materials:
- bib apron
- felt
- felt scraps
- glue gun
- scissors
- Velcro™

DIRECTIONS:
Cut pieces from felt to make a story scene similar to the one below. Glue in place. Cut characters from felt to use on the apron for telling "Little Red Riding Hood," "The Three Billy Goats Gruff," or "The Three Little Pigs." (See patterns on pages 164, 166, 168, and 169.) Glue a small piece of Velcro™ (hook side) to the back of each piece so it will stick better to the felt. Tell different stories to the children, then let them retell the stories using the apron.

ADAPTATION:
Hang the apron on the back of a chair, or pin it to a bulletin board.

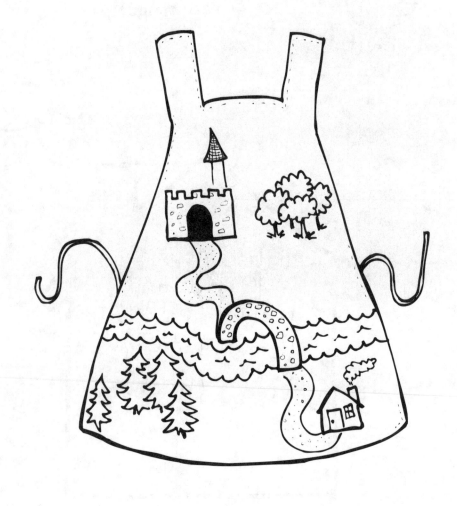

BOOKS
&
BEYOND
ACTIVITIES

Reading Together

Skill:
making connections between spoken word and print

Materials:
- language experience charts
- markers
- big books
- pointer

DIRECTIONS:
Print words to nursery rhymes, poems, chants, or finger plays on language experience charts. (Big books may also be used.) Try one of the suggested techniques below to engage children in reading together.

Echo Reading - The teacher reads a line or phrase, then the children repeat what the teacher has read.

Choral Reading - The teacher and children read the words in unison.

Back and Forth - The teacher reads a line, then the children read a line.

Word Clap - The teacher introduces one or two words before the reading begins. Whenever the teacher comes to those words, he/she pauses while the children clap and supply the missing word.

ADAPTATIONS:
Encourage children to use some of the above techniques when doing "paired reading" with a friend.

HINT! Point to the words with your finger or a pointer (see pages 50 and 122) to help children focus visually and develop directionality.

Book Buddies

DIRECTIONS:

Pair children into "buddy" partners. Let each pair choose a book and look at it together. You might suggest they take turns "reading" or talking about the pictures. Encourage them to retell, in their own words, stories that you have previously read.

ADAPTATIONS:

Set aside a special time each day or week for "book buddies" to read together.

Choose one child each day to be the teacher's "book buddy."

Pair a class of younger children with an upper-grade class in your school. Match an older child with a younger child and let them read together once a week for 15-20 minutes. The older students could also create books or write original stories for their younger partner.

Give children paper and pencils and let them be "writing buddies." They could also be "art buddies" and color or paint pictures together.

Have a book "show and tell" where children bring in books and summarize them for classmates.

HINT! Partner activities are an excellent way to encourage peer tutoring. A child who has mastered skills can often help a struggling learner.

<u>Skills:</u>
motivation to read; retelling a story

<u>Materials:</u>
• books
• magazines
• printed material

Authors, Illustrators, and Comments

Skill:
understanding concepts about books

Materials:
• paper
• pens
• pencils
• class-made books

DIRECTIONS:

Explain that people who write books are called "authors," and people who draw pictures for books are called "illustrators." Each time you read a book to the class, tell them who the author and illustrator are. When you make class books, add an extra page to the beginning of the book. Write: "This book was written by ____" or "This book was written and illustrated by ____." You can also title the page "Authors" or "Authors and Illustrators." Let the children sign their names on the page to indicate their participation.

Include an extra page at the end of the home-made books for "comments and compliments." If children take the book home to share with their family, or if other people read the book, ask them to sign their name and write what they thought about the book.

ADAPTATIONS:

Encourage the children to sign their names as "author and illustrator" when they make individual books.

Include a dedication page, copyright date, and a publisher on class books.

HINT! Always write "The End" on the last page of books you make. It's something that every child in your room will be able to read!

Turn the Page

DIRECTIONS:

Sing the following song to prepare children for story time or independent reading:

Turn the Page (Tune: "This Old Man")

Here we go, get a book,	(Put hands out in front of you.)
Open it up and have a look.	(Open up hands to make a book.)
Turn the page and you will see	(Pretend to turn the page.)
Reading's fun for you and me!	
Turn the page - read, read, read.	(Pretend to turn pages in a book.)
Turn the page - read, read, read.	
Close your book and put it away,	(Close hands and put them in your lap.)
We'll read more another day.	

Have children demonstrate how to take books and magazines and turn the page.

ADAPTATION:

Give children books and ask them to show you the front, back, and top of the book.

HINT! Be sure to turn the page in the opposite direction (right to left, not left to right) so it will be the correct way from the children's point of view.

Skills:
understanding concepts about books; how to turn pages in a book

Materials:
· classroom books or magazines

A Message from Our Mascot

Skill:
motivation to read

Materials:
- dry erase board
- markers
- chalkboard or language experience chart
- stuffed toy or puppet

DIRECTIONS:

Choose a stuffed animal or puppet to be your classroom mascot. Introduce the mascot by wrapping it up as a gift. Explain that you have a special friend who will help them learn how to read. Tell the children that the mascot can't talk, but it can write them messages. Have the children suggest names for the mascot and vote on their favorite name. Each day before the children arrive, write the date and a short message from the mascot on the board. (You might say something positive about the class, tell about a special activity, give a birthday greeting, ask a question, or leave a new book, game, or snack for the children.) Place the mascot by the message and explain that the mascot "wrote" them something. Tell the children they'll have to help you "read" it to see what the mascot has said. Have the children follow along as you read the message. Choose individual children to come up and point to the words as you re-read it together.

Good morning friends!
Today is Friday, March 5th.
Here's one of my favorite stories about a hippopotamus.
I hope you'll like it. Ms. Davis has a new game to teach you.
Have a great day!
Your Friend,
Max

ADAPTATION:

Let children draw pictures and write messages back to the mascot.

Today is Monday, October 25.

I hope you brought some leaves for your art project.
You get to cook a special snack today.

Congratulations to Joan. She has a new baby sister.
Remember to share today.
Your Friend,
Max

Book Shopping

DIRECTIONS:

Spread the books out on the floor. Hold up the books one at a time and ask the children what they think each book is about. Why? Tell them that they're going to pretend they are going shopping for a book. Choose a child and hand him or her the shopping bag. Describe one of the books on display, then have the child select the book that he or she thinks matches your description and put it in the bag. Continue to select different children to "shop" for books. Conclude by having children talk about what kind of books they like.

ADAPTATIONS:

Use different types of printed materials for this activity. For example, you could use a phone book, cookbook, newspaper, television guide, nature magazine, dictionary, atlas, and so forth. Describe different needs, then have children select the book that would provide you with the information you need.

Ask children to sort books that are "real" and "pretend."

Have children do graphs of their favorite kinds of books or of their favorite author.

Who's Your Favorite Author?						
Authors	1	2	3	4	5	6
Carle	X	X	X			
Rey	X					
Marshall	X	X	X	X		
Sendak	X	X				
Freeman	X	X	X	X	X	

Story Map

DIRECTIONS:

Draw a story map on the poster board similar to the one below. Laminate it or cover with clear contact paper. After reading a book to the children, have them recall the information using the story map as a guide. Write in the information with an erasable marker so the story map can be used repeatedly.

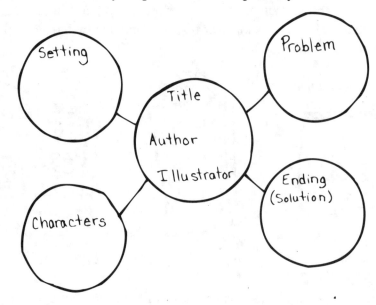

ADAPTATIONS:

Use other graphic organizers to foster visualization and learning.

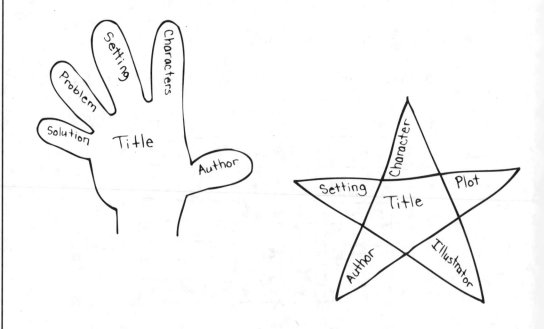

Story Stepping Stones

DIRECTIONS:

Cut paper in the shape of stepping stones. Write the parts of a book shown below on each stone. Place these on the floor and cover with clear contact paper. After reading a book to the children, let them "step" on each stone, giving the information indicated.

ADAPTATIONS:

Let different children stand on each stone and tell about their part in the story.

Write "problem," "solution," "what would happen next," or other elements about stories on the stones.

HINT! Laminate stepping stones, then just spread them out on the floor when you want to do this activity.

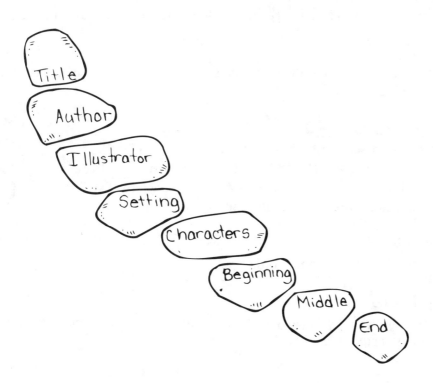
Skill:
recognizing parts of a story

Materials:
- construction paper
- scissors
- markers
- clear contact paper

Story Recall

DIRECTIONS:

After reading stories or other information to children, sharpen their recall skills with one of these activities:

Smart Art

Ask children to draw or paint pictures about books you have read to them. Let them make paper bag puppets, stick puppets, or sock puppets. Give them clay to make their favorite character or, for an extension activity, provide them with other art media.

Skits

Have children act out stories they enjoy for classmates. Well-known folktales that have a simple plot and a few characters work best.

Riddles

Make up riddles about characters or events in the story for the children to solve, then let them make up their own riddles for classmates.

Ask Me a Question

Allow children to ask the teacher or classmates questions about material read.

Favorite Scenes

Have the children find their favorite scene in the book and talk about the picture or event to friends.

Compare and Contrast

Compare and contrast different books you read to the class. Ask questions such as: "How is this story similar to....?" "How is this story different from....?" "How were the characters alike?" "Have we read another story by this author?"

Order, Please

Recall events in sequential order.

Story Journal

Have children keep a "story journal" where they can draw pictures or write about books shared in class.

Class Books

DIRECTIONS:

Choose from the titles below to make a book:

My Family
I Wish . . .
Monsters and Things That Scare Us
Fun on a Rainy Day
If I Were the President (or Teacher, or Principal)
If Shoes Could Talk
Animals We'd Like to Be
When I Grow Up
My Worst (or Best) Day Ever
Celebrate! (Family Celebrations)
Our Heroes
Dreams
The Best Thing about Me
What Color Are You Inside?
Things to be Happy About
If I Could Be Anyone, I Would Be . . .
What a Wonderful World!
Things That Bug Me

Explain the title of the book and encourage the class to discuss what it means. Give each child a piece of paper and ask them to draw a picture or write a story to go in the book. (Let younger children dictate their story to an adult.) Fold the construction paper in half to make a cover for the book, then staple the children's pages inside. Write the title on the front cover and let several children decorate it. Read the book to the class, then place it in your library.

ADAPTATIONS:

Create class books around themes, field trips, holidays, current events, etc.

Allow children to check out class books and take them home to share.

Pass around class books to other classrooms in your school.

Make a "Get Well" book for children who are ill for an extended period. You can also make "Thank You" books for school helpers or volunteers.

Skills:
writing, creativity

Materials:
• construction paper (12" x 18")
• $8\frac{1}{2}$" x 11" paper
• crayons
• markers
• pencils
• stapler

I Can Read

Skill:
reading (using environmental print)

Materials:
- construction paper (cut 8" x 6")
- magazines
- catalogs
- newspapers
- crayons
- scissors
- glue
- hole punch
- yarn

DIRECTIONS:

Give each child five pieces of construction paper. Have them punch two holes in the left side of each sheet, then tie the pages together with yarn. Let the children write "I Can Read" on the cover. (Encourage them to write their name as the author.) Next, ask the children to cut out words they can read from magazines, newspapers, or catalogs, and glue them in their book. Have the children read their books and share them with each other.

ADAPTATIONS:

Send the books home with a note to the parents asking them to help their child continue to add to their books by finding more words they can read around their house.

Have children make similar books by cutting out letters or numerals they can identify from magazines and newspapers.

Make "shopping bag books" with sacks from restaurants and stores. After collecting sacks, punch a hole in the left-hand corner of each bag. Tie together with a piece of yarn or string. Have the children "read" the sacks as they identify the logos.

Use paper plates and wrappers to make a "We Eat" book. Glue a different package on each plate, then put the plates together with a book ring.

Baggie Book

DIRECTIONS:

Place an object in each baggie. Put a sticker label on the top of each bag and label the objects. Lay the bags on top of each other. Poke two holes in the side of each bag, then attach together with pipe cleaners or bread ties. Ask children to name the objects in the bags. Explain that the word on each page tells what the object is. Can they read the word? Praise children for "reading."

ADAPTATIONS:

Cut construction paper to fit in the baggies. Glue children's photographs or self-portraits on the construction paper and label with their names. Put in the bags, zip, and attach the bags together with yarn or ribbon.

Recycle torn-up books with zipper bags. Get gallon-size bags and place torn pages from the old book in the bags. Sequence the pages, then attach bags together with pipe cleaners.

Calendars, brochures, magazine pictures, children's drawings, and greeting cards can also be used to make baggie books.

Write words or sentences to go along with each picture before sealing them in the bags.

Skill:
reading labels

Materials:
- four to five zipper sandwich bags
- sticker labels
- markers
- small flat objects (feather, leaf, crayon, balloon, bandage)
- pipe cleaner (cut in half) or bread ties
- hole punch

Alphabet Sing-Along Book

Skills:
recognizing letters; visual matching

Materials:
- paper
- crayons or markers
- magnetic letters
- hole punch
- book rings
- construction paper

DIRECTIONS:

Trace around one of the magnetic letters on the bottom of each page. Distribute these to the children and ask them to draw something that starts with the letter on their page. (Give them "hints" or suggest they look around the room for ideas.) Write this sentence on the bottom of each page: "[letter] is for [object]." Collect the children's drawings and put them in alphabetical order. Make a cover for the book from construction paper. Add an author's page and comment page to the book. Punch two holes on the side of each page, then put them together with book rings. Read over the book with the children. Go back through it again and sing it to the tune of "Twinkle, Twinkle, Little Star."

ADAPTATIONS:

Place the book and magnetic letters in a learning center. Demonstrate how to match the plastic letters with the letter outlines in the book.

Have the children draw their pictures with a black pen or crayon, then run off a copy for each child. Put the pages in a construction paper cover and let the children decorate it. Send it home with a note to the parents explaining how to sing the song and use the book with their child.

Tag-Along Book

DIRECTIONS:

Take several sheets of copy paper and place them on top of the construction paper. Fold the construction paper in half to make a book and staple along the fold. Let the children write stories or draw pictures in the book. (Younger children can dictate their stories to an adult.) Encourage children to write a title on the front and add their name as the "author." Punch two holes near the staples and attach a pipe cleaner for a handle as shown. These books can "tag along" home with the children so they can share them with their families.

ADAPTATION:

Cut the front and back off gift bags. (Leave handles attached.) Cut paper to fit inside and staple at the top. Children can write stories or draw pictures on the paper. Hang in the classroom library.

Skill:
creating an interest in books through writing

Materials:
- construction paper (9" x 11")
- copy paper (8½" x 11")
- stapler
- hole punch
- crayons
- markers
- pipe cleaners

Big Book Joke Book

DIRECTIONS:

Divide the students into pairs and ask them to think of a joke or riddle. Give each pair half a piece of poster board. Have them write or dictate the riddle on the front side; have them draw the answer to their riddle on the back. Make a cover for the book that says, "The Big Book Joke Book." Put the pages together, hole punch, and attach with book rings or pipe cleaners. Read over the book with the class, then put it in your library.

ADAPTATIONS:

Make a big "Knock, Knock, Who's There?" riddle book.

Let children make their own individual riddle books and share them with friends.

Involve children in making other big books about themes, projects, animals, foods, or other topics of interest.

Tell the President

DIRECTIONS:

Put the paper in the notebook. Tape a picture of the President to the front and label the notebook "Tell the President." Tie a pencil or pen to the string and attach it to the notebook. Explain to the class that when they have a complaint, problem, or suggestion they would like to make, they should write it down in the notebook. (For children who can't write, tell them just to draw a picture about it.)

ADAPTATIONS:

Create a "Kindness Book" for children. When you catch them doing a kind deed, record their name in this book.

Make a book of class rules. Ask each child to draw a picture of a rule he or she thinks is important; dictate or write a sentence to go with it. Put the pictures together into a "Class Rule Book." Refer to the book when children misbehave, and have them "read" over the rule with you.

HINT! This is a great way to distract children from tattling and to encourage them to use print.

Imagination Felt Book

Skill:

telling a story in sequence

Materials:
- 9" x 12" pieces of felt (in a variety of colors)
- felt scraps
- needle and thread
- glue gun
- scissors

DIRECTIONS:

Take five to six pieces of felt and sew them together along the left side using a blanket stitch. Cut a pocket out of felt and glue it to the front cover. Make trees, animals, houses, vehicles, people, and other small objects from felt scraps and put them in the pocket. Let the children take the felt pieces and create their own original stories on the pages in the book.

ADAPTATIONS:

Cut out felt letters that children can put together to make words in the book.

Cut out numerals and small shapes from felt. Have the children use these to make sets, reproduce patterns, or tell number stories.

Teddy Bear, Teddy Bear

DIRECTIONS:

Teach the children the rhyme below. Demonstrate the different movements with the toy bear. Have the children stand and follow along with the movements as the bear does them.

Teddy Bear Rhyme

Teddy bear, teddy bear, turn around.
Teddy bear, teddy bear, touch the ground.
Teddy bear, teddy bear, read the news.
Teddy bear, teddy bear, tie your shoes.
Teddy bear, teddy bear, go upstairs.
Teddy bear, teddy bear, say your prayers.
Teddy bear, teddy bear, turn off the light.
Teddy bear, teddy bear, say, "Good night!"

ADAPTATIONS:

Let the children take the bear and do different movements with him. The other children fill in the blank to describe what the bear is doing. For example, "Teddy bear, teddy bear, clap your hands," or "Teddy bear, teddy bear, jump up and down."

 Sing the teddy bear chant to the tune of "Twinkle, Twinkle, Little Star." Add this final verse: "Teddy bear, teddy bear, I love you, and I hope you love me, too."

Make a book similar to the one on the following page. Encourage the children to "read" the book as they say the rhyme.

Let the children make their own teddy bear books to take home.

Teddy Bear Book

DIRECTIONS:

Write one line to the "Teddy Bear" chant on each page. Cut out nine bears from brown felt or tagboard. Glue the bears according to the directions below so that the children can manipulate them to go along with the words. Hole punch the side of each page and put them together with book rings.

1. Title page: Teddy Bear, Teddy Bear

2. "Teddy bear, teddy bear, turn around."
   (Glue down only the right paw and foot so the bear can "turn around.")

3. "Teddy bear, teddy bear, touch the ground."
   (Put glue only on the bottom half of the bear so it can bend over.)

4. "Teddy bear, teddy bear, read the news."
   (Put glue on the bottom of a small piece of newspaper so it can fold up and down.)

5. "Teddy bear, teddy bear, tie your shoes."
   (Poke holes and thread through string.)

6. "Teddy bear, teddy bear, climb the stairs."
   (Cut stair slits in the page. Glue a bear to the craft stick so it can move up and down the stairs.)

7. "Teddy bear, teddy bear, say your prayers."
   (Cut in a little on the arms and don't glue down so they can bend in.)

8. "Teddy bear, teddy bear, turn off the light."
   (Draw a lamp and attach a piece of string.)

9. "Teddy bear, teddy bear, say, 'Good night.' "
   (Glue the bottom of a small piece of fabric on the bed so you can cover up the bear.)

PATTERN FOR TEDDY BEAR BOOK

(Cut out nine from tagboard or brown felt.)

Classroom Yellow Pages

Skill:
repeating a telephone number

Materials:
- front and back cover from the yellow pages phone book
- paper
- markers or crayons
- hole punch
- yarn
- play phone

DIRECTIONS:
Remind the children to learn their phone numbers several days before introducing this activity. Ask them to think of situations when it would be important to know their phone number. Give each child a piece of paper and ask them to draw their picture. Encourage them to write their name at the top and dictate their phone number for an adult to write at the bottom. Place the children's pictures between the covers from the yellow pages of the phone book. Punch two holes in the side of each page and tie them together with a piece of yarn. Demonstrate how to find a friend's name, then match up the numerals on the phone to call them. Let the children take turns role playing as they call friends. Place the book in your library or in the housekeeping area.

ADAPTATIONS:
Use photographs of the children to make this book.

Put paper and a pencil by the classroom yellow pages so the children can copy their friends' numbers and call them at home.

Make a photocopy of this book for each child to take home.

Make a "Class Address Book" by having each child draw a picture of his or her home. Let them dictate their address to an adult.

HINT! If children do not have a phone or have a number that is unlisted, use the school's phone number so they don't feel left out.

How to Make a Peanut Butter Sandwich

DIRECTIONS:

Cut bread, peanut butter, and jelly from felt or construction paper using the patterns on the following page. Make a "How to Make a Peanut Butter Sandwich" book similar to the one below. Hole punch the sides and put the pages together with book rings. Demonstrate how to "read" the book and follow the directions to make a sandwich. Let the children play with this activity independently or in small groups.

ADAPTATIONS:

Make similar activities where children can make a hamburger, pizza, banana split, etc.

Skills:
following directions; placing items in sequence

Materials:
- felt (beige, brown, purple)
- white paper
- markers
- hole punch
- scissors
- book rings

BREAD

Cut several out of beige felt. (You will need <u>twice</u> as much bread as you do peanut butter or jelly.)

JELLY

Cut several out of purple felt.

PEANUT BUTTER

Cut several out of brown felt.

Flip Book

DIRECTIONS:

Make flip books for children using the pattern on the following page. Fold the paper in half, then cut up to the fold on the dotted lines. After reading a story to the children, guide them in recalling the main events of the story in sequential order: "What happened first?" "What happened next?" "What happened then?" "How did the story end?" Give each child a flip book and show them how to lift the flaps one at a time to draw pictures of what happened in the story. Let them share their books with a partner.

Skills:
sequencing; recall

Materials:
• crayons
• colored pencils
• copy of flip book on following page
• scissors

ADAPTATIONS:

Use flip books for children to recall what happened when they went on a field trip, directions for a cooking activity, or other events.

Have children make up original stories with flip books.

Use flip books to make rhyming games or math games, or to reinforce beginning sounds.

HINT! After you demonstrate several times how to make flip books, many children will be able to construct their own.

1

2

3

5

fold

Little "I Can Read" Books

DIRECTIONS:

Take one of the copies and fold it in half with the print side out.

Fold it into fourths.

Fold it into eighths.

Open so it is folded in half. Fold the bottom edge lengthwise up to the fold on one side.

Turn over and bring the bottom edge on the other side to the fold.

cut down fold

stop

Cut down halfway on the middle folded line.

Hold hands on fold, then bring down.

Wrap the pages around to make a little book.

Make one for each child and have them follow along as they practice reading it. Encourage them to take home their books and "read" them to their families.

ADAPTATIONS:

Make little books about colors, shapes, letters, numerals, a cooking activity, a field trip, dinosaurs, or other things children are interested in.

Let children make their own little books to write friends' names in, draw pictures about a story, etc.

Skill:
reading simple sentences

Materials:
- photocopies of the books on the following pages
- scissors
- crayons

THE WHEELS ON THE BUS

The horn on the bus goes beep, beep, beep.

The lights on the bus go blink, blink, blink.

The children on the bus go up and down.

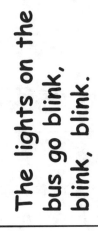

The doors on the bus go open and shut.

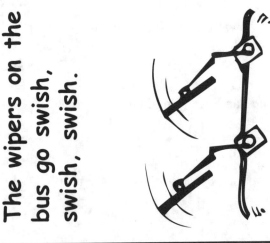

The driver on the bus goes, "Move on back."

The wipers on the bus go swish, swish, swish.

THE WHEELS ON THE BUS

The wheels on the bus go round and round.

An embarrassed zebra.

What's black and white and red all over?

What has eyes but can't see?

An umbrella.

A potato.

What goes up when the rain comes down?

LITTLE JOKE BOOK

A hot dog.

What kind of dog has no tail?

HA!

HA!

Ha!

Classroom Alphabet Books

DIRECTIONS:

   Make alphabet books similar to those below with the children to encourage their interest in print and letters.

Sweet ABC

DIRECTIONS:

   Write a letter of the alphabet on each page and put them together in alphabetical order. Make a cover for the book and write "Sweet Letters" on it. Hole punch and tie the book together with yarn. Ask children to bring in gum or candy wrappers and glue them on the appropriate page. Keep the book on a special shelf so children can add to it through the year. Encourage children to "read" the different candy labels.

ADAPTATION:

   Make a similar book using cereal or food logos.

Finger Talk Alphabet

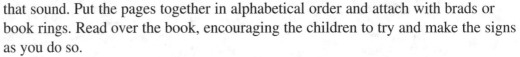

DIRECTIONS:

   Let the children choose their favorite sign language letter and glue it on a piece of paper. Ask them to print the letter and draw a picture of objects that begin with that sound. Put the pages together in alphabetical order and attach with brads or book rings. Read over the book, encouraging the children to try and make the signs as you do so.

ADAPTATION:

   Make a similar book using the Braille alphabet. Glue lentils or dried peas on paper to make each letter.

Textured ABC's

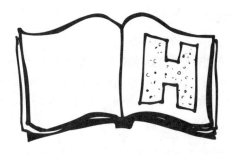

DIRECTIONS:

Make letters from textured materials and glue them on the paper. Arrange the pages in order, hole punch, and bind with book rings. Demonstrate how to trace over the letters with your finger as you say them.

ADAPTATION:

Assign each child a different letter to decorate with his or her parents at home. Put the pages together for a class book.

Theme Alphabet Books

DIRECTIONS:

Make alphabet books that relate to different classroom themes or seasons. For example, you could make a book of animals, insects, feelings, types of transportation, foods, toys, signs of spring, and so forth. Give each child a piece of paper and let them choose a letter. Give them markers, crayons, paints, and other art media to create their page for the book. Put the pages together, make a cover from construction paper, and write the title. Add an "author's and illustrator's" page for the children to sign. Hole punch and tie together with string or book rings.

ADAPTATIONS:

Let children check these books out to take home and share with their families.

Make a "Friend Alphabet Book" by using children's photographs or self-portraits for the letter that their name begins with. If you have no names that begin with a particular letter, then use storybook characters, sports figures, or other famous people's names.

Materials:
- felt
- sandpaper
- glue
- colored rice
- glitter
- yarn
- heavy paper
- hole punch
- book rings

Materials:
- construction paper
- copy paper
- crayons
- markers
- art supplies
- hole punch
- string or book rings

Materials:
- construction paper
- scissors
- paper
- stapler
- markers
- crayons
- pens
- pencils
- magazines
- glue

Materials:
- paper
- marker
- crayons
- construction paper
- hole punch
- ribbon

Sound Books

DIRECTIONS:

Make books for different letters as you focus on them. Cut paper in the shape of the letter and staple in a construction paper cover. Keep books on a shelf with crayons, pens, glue, and magazines. Encourage children to draw pictures, write words, or cut out magazine letters (that begin with that sound) and add to the book.

Camouflage ABC's

DIRECTIONS:

Write a large letter with the marker in the middle of each page. Pass out a letter to each child. Talk about what the word "camouflage" means. Ask the children to look at their letter and see if the shape resembles something else. Have them turn their letter upside down and all around. Challenge them to "camouflage" their letter by turning it into that object. Put the pages in alphabetical order between construction paper to make a book. Hole punch and tie with ribbon. Play a guessing game as you read over the book together and try to "find" each letter hidden on the page.

ADAPTATION:

See if children can create something from their letter that begins with the sound that letter makes.

Bookmarks

DIRECTIONS:

Make up a story about reading a book and having to stop in the middle of it. Ask children what you could do to help mark your spot in the book. Lead them into a discussion of bookmarks and why people use them. Demonstrate how to make one of the bookmarks below, then allow the children to make their own.

Envelope Bookmark

DIRECTIONS:

Cut off the corner of the envelope as shown. Color a face or design on it, then insert it over the corner of a book page to mark your place.

Mouse Tail

DIRECTIONS:

Fold a piece of construction paper in half to cut out a heart. Insert an 8" piece of yarn inside for a tail and glue the sides together. Add eyes, ears, a nose, and whiskers. Insert the mouse's tail in the book.

Materials:
- envelopes
- scissors
- markers or crayons

Materials:
- construction paper
- scissors
- glue
- yarn
- markers or crayons

Materials:
- burlap
- felt scraps
- scissors
- glue

Materials:
- clear contact paper or self-laminating sheets
- small leaves or flowers

Materials:
- construction paper
- scissors
- crayons

Fabric Bookmark

DIRECTIONS:
Cut burlap into 2½" by 8" strips. Unravel burlap ½" from the top, bottom, and sides. Decorate by gluing on felt scraps.

ADAPTATION:
Cut felt and imitation leather into 2" x 7" strips and use as bookmarks.

Nature Bookmark

DIRECTIONS:
Cut two pieces of 2½" x 7" contact or self-laminating paper. Take children outside to collect small leaves, flowers, and petals. Peel the back off one strip and arrange the natural objects on the sticky side. Cover with the second strip to seal in place.

ADAPTATION:
Use sequins, glitter, and foil paper in a similar manner to make a "shiny" bookmark.

Bookworms

DIRECTIONS:
Cut paper into the shape of bookworms using the pattern below. Let children decorate with crayons.

PARENTS PLUS!

PARENT
PARTNERSHIPS

LITERACY IN THE
HOME

TAKE-HOME
ACTIVITIES

QUALITY TIME

Mom and Me

Learning My Way

Materials:
- copy of letter on the following page

DIRECTIONS:
Plan monthly meetings with parents. Explain skills you are working on at school and give them examples of how they can reinforce these at home. Point out learning centers in your classroom and describe what children learn from playing with the different materials. Among other activities, have parents play with blocks, paint a picture, or work with manipulatives, then ask them to reflect on what they learned.

Use anecdotal records, portfolios, and other work samples at conferences to validate children's progress.

Send home a copy of the letter and poem on the following page for parents to read.

ADAPTATION:
The more you share with parents and help them understand your program philosophy and goals, the stronger the partnership you will create with them. Invite them into your room to volunteer, send home articles and newsletters, and make videos of your children acting out stories, dictating a language experience chart, talking about a book, and so forth.

Parents Plus!

Dear Parents:

Often someone will ask, "When is my child going to learn how to read?" Learning to read begins from the moment of birth and continues throughout childhood. All children learn to read in their own special way and at different times. The important thing to recognize is that all the experiences your child has every day—from dressing themselves, to singing a song, to telling you about their day—contribute to laying a foundation and building skills and attitudes. Read this poem, then observe your child. Don't you see him/her thinking and trying? Give them your support, encouragement, and TIME. They'll be young only for a little while!

Learning My Way

by Jean Feldman

When I listen to a story or look at books each day,
I'm learning to read in my own special way.
When I sing a song or say a rhyme,
My listening skills will develop on time.
The small muscles I use when I work a puzzle or play with clay
Will help me to write a sentence one day.
When I jump, wiggle, and run the day long,
My muscles and body are growing strong.
When I put away my toys or pass out snacks at school,
I'm really doing my math, too.
Making bubbles in the tub or looking at the sky
Will develop my scientific skills by and by.
My coloring, painting, and gluing may look like a mess,
But they all encourage my creative best.
When you read to me, talk, and listen, too,
I'll learn to love books and language, it's true.
Holding me close, hugs, and quality time,
Show me that you're glad you're mine.
When you accept me for who I am and cherish what I do,
I'll learn to love others and respect them, too.
As you give me choices and let me go,
Into an independent adult I will grow.
Every minute of every new and exciting day,
I'm learning and growing in my own special way.

Visit a Library

DIRECTIONS:

Send home a letter (similar to the one below) that encourages parents to visit their local library.

Dear Parents:

One of the best ways you can interest your children in books and reading is to take them to your neighborhood library. The library is a magical place with books, magazines, reference materials, tapes, videos, computers, and a world they may otherwise never know! Your library has a special story hour for children, as well as other fun programs. You can also find some great resources on parenting or other topics you might be interested in.

Make your child feel responsible with his or her own library card. A special book bag or safe place to store the books in your home will help your child care for library books. So....visit your library soon, and read a book!

Thanks for leading your child to reading!

[Teacher's signature]
Your Child's Teacher

ADAPTATION:

Invite a public librarian to a parent's meeting, or take your class on a field trip to the library.

Special Delivery

DIRECTIONS:

Cut the paper so it fits the outside of the can. Let each child decorate a piece of paper with markers or crayons. (Make sure they also write their name on it.) Glue the paper to the can, then cover with clear adhesive or self-laminating sheets. Make copies of the task cards on the following pages to send home in children's cans.

Explain that the cans contain a "special delivery" for their parents, and they get to play mail carrier and take it home. When their parents open it, there will be a special assignment that they can do together. Remind them to return their empty cans to school the next day so they can get another special assignment.

ADAPTATIONS:

Get feedback from parents on how they are enjoying doing the activities with their children. Ask them to make suggestions of other things to put on the task cards.

Tell the parents to save the task cards to use again with their children.

Materials:
- empty potato chip canisters
- paper
- markers or
- crayons
- glue
- clear adhesive paper
- copies of task cards on the following pages

READ ME A STORY.
TELL ME THE AUTHOR
AND ILLUSTRATOR.

PLAY A GAME WITH ME.

LET'S TAKE A WALK
AND LOOK FOR THINGS
BIGGER THAN ME AND
THINGS SMALLER
THAN ME.

SING A SONG WITH ME.

WORK A PUZZLE
WITH ME.

LET ME COOK
SOMETHING SPECIAL
TO EAT.

TELL ME WHAT YOU
WERE LIKE WHEN YOU
WERE LITTLE. WHAT
WAS YOUR FAVORITE
BOOK?

ASK ME TO FIND
DIFFERENT SHAPES, LIKE
CIRCLES, SQUARES,
TRIANGLES, AND
RECTANGLES.

HELP ME WRITE A
LETTER TO SOMEONE.

GIVE ME A BACK RUB.

ASK ME TO NAME
WORDS THAT RHYME.

LET ME HELP YOU DO A
JOB AROUND THE HOUSE.

HELP ME COUNT THE
NUMBER OF DOORS IN
OUR HOUSE. WHAT
ELSE CAN WE COUNT?

TEACH ME HOW TO ZIP,
BUTTON, SNAP, AND TIE.

TELL ME ABOUT
YOUR JOB.

LET'S SAY SOME
NURSERY RHYMES
TOGETHER.

ASK ME MY NAME,
BIRTHDAY, ADDRESS,
AND PHONE NUMBER.

TEACH ME THE DAYS OF
THE WEEK AND MONTHS
OF THE YEAR.

ACT OUT OPPOSITES,
LIKE "UP AND DOWN,"
"HOT AND COLD,"
"BIG AND LITTLE," ETC.

READ ME A BOOK AND
LEAVE OUT SOME WORDS.
LET ME GUESS WHAT
THEY ARE.

Color Posters

Materials:
- poster board or foam board
- glue gun

DIRECTIONS:
Send home a letter similar to the one below that asks children to bring in objects of a particular color to school. Glue the objects to a poster board or foam board and label. Hang in the classroom and add other color posters as you make them.

Dear Parents:

We are making a poster at school with objects that are (color). We would like each child to bring in a small object or picture of something in that color. We will glue these on our poster and hang it in our classroom, so please send objects you don't want returned. Ask your child to find other objects that are (color) around your house, outdoors, in foods, on clothes, etc.

Thanks!

[Teacher's signature]
Your Child's Teacher

ADAPTATION:
Make posters of different shapes, letters, or other concepts.

HINT! A low-temp glue gun works well for securing heavy posters to your classroom wall, but test it on a small area first to make sure it doesn't damage walls.

Pet Tales

DIRECTIONS:

Choose a stuffed animal that you think the children would enjoy. Have the children name the pet, then place it in the cloth bag along with the notebook, crayons, and pen. Write a letter similar to the one below and pin it to the front of the notebook. Each day select a different child to take home the bag and pet. When the child returns the bag to school the next day, read to the class what their parent has written in the notebook.

ADAPTATION:

Add a book, toothbrush, change of clothes, or other "personal" items for the pet.

HINT! Be prepared to do this activity with children who do not get any help at home.

Materials:
- spiral notebook
- pen
- crayons
- stuffed animal
- cloth bag

Letter Bags

Materials:
- paper lunch sacks
- markers

DIRECTIONS:

Write a note home to parents similar to the one below:

Dear Parents,

    Each Monday your child will be bringing home a different "letter bag." Please help your child look around his or her room and find one or two objects that begin with the sound on the front of the sack. The children will share their "letter bags" at school on Tuesday, then they will bring the objects back home. During the week you can reinforce this letter/sound by pointing out the letter on food boxes, on signs, or in books. Play games where you and your child think of all the words you can that start with that sound. Thanks for making learning more meaningful by reinforcing what goes on in school in your home. **You do make a difference!**

[Teacher's signature]
Your Child's Teacher

    Print a different letter on the sacks with a magic marker each week before distributing them to the children.

ADAPTATION:

    Write numerals, colors, or other information on the sacks that parents can reinforce at home.

HINT! Always be ready to help the child who does not get support at home. Put something in their bag at school.

Alphabet Bottles

DIRECTIONS:

Send a note home to parents asking them to create a letter bottle for your classroom collection. They will need a clear plastic bottle (16 oz. works well) and small objects that can be found around the house or yard. Assign each family a different letter. Their challenge is to see how many objects they can find that begin with that sound that will fit in the bottle. When the child returns the bottle to school, glue the lid on. Tape the child's name and his or her letter on the front of the bottle. Have children guess what each object in the bottle is. What other words begin with that sound?

ADAPTATIONS:

Remove the letter on the outside of the bottle and challenge the children to identify the sound the items represent.

Make lists of all the items in the bottle for the children to "read" and find.

For younger children, ask parents to create color bottles. Assign each family a different color and ask them to collect objects of that color to go in the bottle.

Materials:
- plastic bottles
- common objects found around the house

Homework Journal

DIRECTIONS:

Prepare a homework journal for each child by having them decorate the outside of a pocket folder. Each week make a list similar to the one below of activities parents can do with their children to reinforce learning at home. Send journals home on Monday and ask the parents to return them on Friday.

Introduce the "homework journal" to parents at your orientation meeting at the beginning of the year. Write weekly notes to parents in the journals to thank them for participating in their child's education.

HINT! Keep assignments short, meaningful, simple, and FUN! Save journals for review at conference time.

Week of _____ Our theme this week is _____.

Skills we are working on are_____

_____.

DAY	ASSIGNMENT	CHECK OFF
Monday	Count the number of trees in your yard. How many different trees do you have? Can you identify them?	_____
Tuesday	Make a list of all the things around your house that are made from wood. Draw pictures to illustrate your list. Bring the list to school with you on Wednesday.	_____
Wednesday	Name words that are opposites, such as up-down, top-bottom, left-right. How many opposites can you think of? Can you act them out?	_____
Thursday	Read a story with your parents. Can you name the author and illustrator of the book? Retell the story in your own words.	_____

*Coming Attractions! Next week we will be focusing on weather. Watch a weather report with your child on television, or look at the "weather watch" in the newspaper.

Comments:

Take-Home Kits

DIRECTIONS:

Make "take-home kits" similar those below, and allow one child to take home a kit each night and interact with their parents.

Materials:
- cloth bags
- backpacks
- briefcases
- lunch boxes and suggested items

Story Kit:

Put a book and stuffed animal in a bag. Include words for a song, fingerplay, or game that relates to the story.

Writing Kit:

Add paper, sticky notes, pens, colored pencils, envelopes, notepads, stickers, chalkboard, chalk, junk mail, and other writing materials to a briefcase for writing fun.

Math Kit:

Place a ruler, calculator, dice, counting toys, minute timer, deck of playing cards, measuring cups, paper, pencil, play money, or toy clock in a lunch box.

Art Kit:

Fill a backpack with crayons, markers, water colors, paint brushes, construction paper, glue, scissors, paper plates, lunch sacks, cardboard rollers, and other media to encourage creativity.

Dramatic Kit:

Put puppets, flannel board pieces, story headbands (see page 160), or dress-up clothes in a bag for children to pretend play.

Science Kit:

Use a lunch box to hold a magnifying glass, magnet, field guide books, binoculars (made from two toilet paper rolls taped together), plastic glove (for collecting specimens), and zip baggies (to hold specimens).

Homework Bags

Materials:
- fabric (solid)
- thick yarn
- markers
- scissors
- sewing machine thread
- crayons
- blank books
- stickers
- junk mail
- pencils
- envelopes
- mini-books (see next few pages)
- play dough
- pasta with holes
- cereal box puzzle
- chalk
- etc.

DIRECTIONS:

Cut two 10" x 12" rectangles for each bag. Fold back 1" on the top of both pieces of fabric. To make a casing, sew one-half inch down from the top straight across as shown. Place the two front sides of the material together, then sew around the three outer edges. (Do not sew above the casing.) Turn the fabric right side out. Cut an 18" piece of yarn and thread it through the casing. Knot the ends of the yarn together. Place a piece of cardboard in the bags, then let the children decorate them with markers. Remove the cardboard, fill the bags with some of the materials listed below, then send them home once a week with the children.

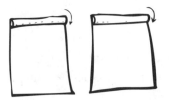

a. Add a blank book and a box of crayons. (A blank book can be made by folding two pieces of paper in half and stapling them together on the fold.)

b. Plastic bag with play dough and the recipe. (See page 125.)

c. Puzzle made from a cereal box. (See page 130.)

d. Chalk with a note about drawing shapes and writing your child's name on the sidewalk.

e. Mini-book. (See page 221.)

f. Pencil (seasonal or colored are fun) and sticky notes.

g. Stickers and paper.

h. Envelopes and blank paper cut in half.

i. Junk mail and pen or pencil.

j. Bag of pasta with holes and a piece of yarn to string a necklace. (Plastic straws can also be cut up into ½" pieces and used to make a necklace.)

k. Words to songs, chants, nursery rhymes, or poems children have learned at school.

l. Mazes, hidden pictures, puzzles, jokes, recipes, etc.

ADAPTATIONS:
Large heavy-duty zip bags can be used in place of drawstring bags.

DIRECTIONS:
Cut these pages apart along the dotted lines, then put together and staple to make a mini-book.

I Like

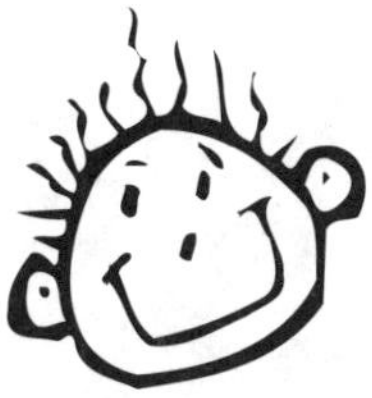

Parents, in this book encourage your child to draw things he or she likes or to cut them out of an old magazine and glue them on the pages. Label your child's "likes" and read over the words together.

2

I like food.

3

I like my family.

4

I like colors.

I like friends.

I like animals.

I like toys.

(Have your child draw pictures.)

NURSERY RHYMES

Parents, read over the
nursery rhymes in this
book with your child.
Can you think of any
other nursery rhymes
you could teach him or her?

Jack and Jill went up the hill
To fetch a pail of water.
Jack fell down and broke his crown
And Jill came tumbling after.

Hickory, dickory dock.
The mouse ran up the clock.
The clock struck ONE.
The mouse ran down.
Hickory, dickory dock.

Humpty Dumpty sat on a wall.
Humpty Dumpty had a great fall.
All the King's horses
And all the King's men
Couldn't put Humpty
Together again.

Little Miss Muffet sat on her tuffet
Eating her curds and whey.
Along came a spider
Who sat down beside her
And frightened Miss Muffet away!

Hey, diddle, diddle,
The cat and the fiddle,
The cow jumped over the moon.
The little dog laughed to see such a sport,
And the dish ran away with the spoon.

7

Jack be nimble,
Jack be quick,
Jack jump over
The candlestick.

Mary had a little lamb
Whose fleece was white as snow.
And everywhere that Mary went
The lamb was sure to go.

APPENDIX

LETTER PATTERNS

SHAPE PATTERNS

ALPHABET PICTURES

AMERICAN MANUAL ALPHABET

RHYME PICTURES

REBUS PICTURES

MANUSCRIPT WRITING GUIDE

Aa	Bb	Cc
Dd	Ee	Ff
Gg	Hh	Ii
Jj	Kk	Ll

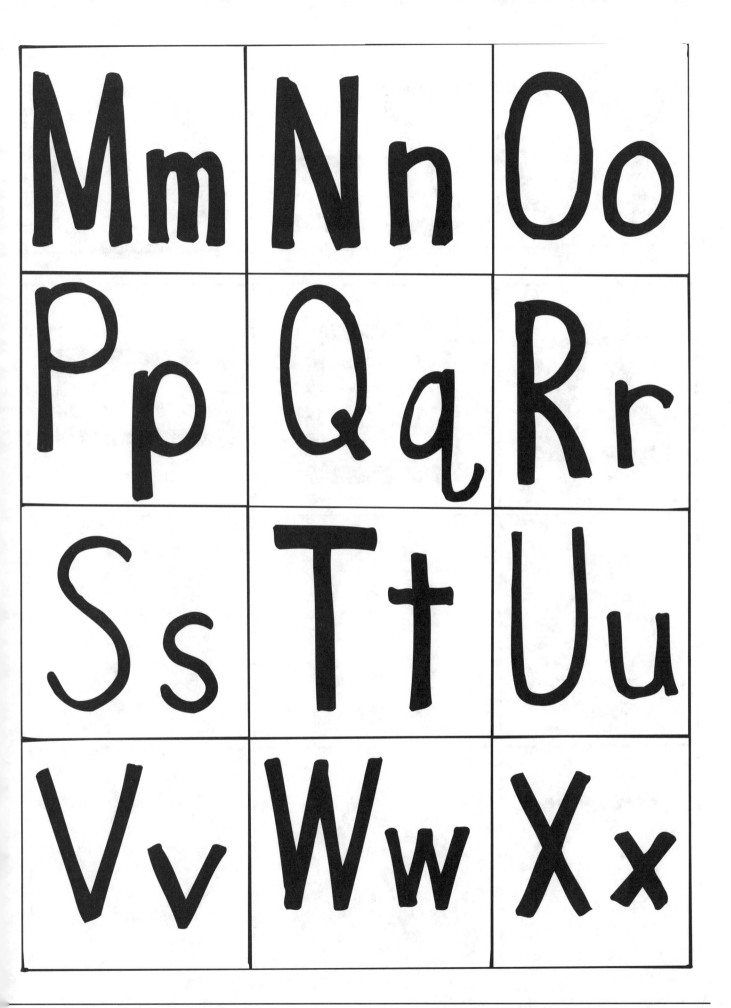

Y y   Z z   ◯

△   ▢   ▭

◇   ⬭   ☽

♡   ☆   ⬡

apple

ball

cat

dog

elephant

fish

goat

horse

iguana

jump rope

kite

lion

monkey

net

octopus

pig

queen

rabbit

sun

turtle

umbrella

violin

wagon

X-ray

yo yo

Zipper

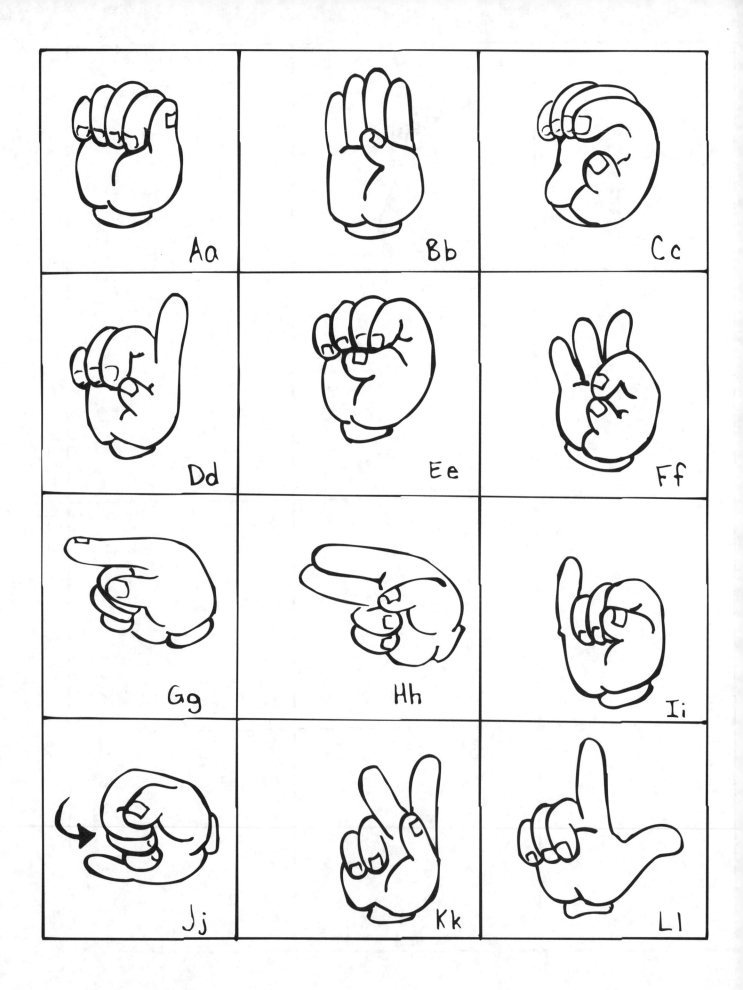

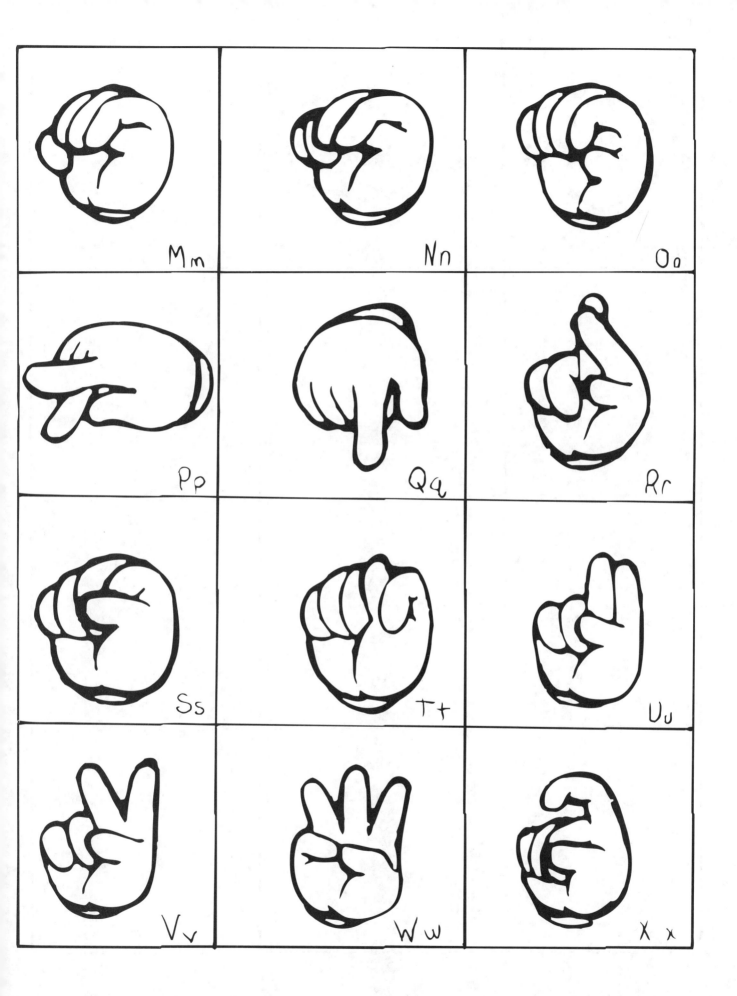

Yy

Zz

rug

car

pan

bug

star

man

moon

mouse

bat

spoon

house

hat

run	hop	fly
cat	rabbit	boy
eat	swim	crawl
bird	sleep	walk

dance

fish

girl

jump

skip

dog

horse

paint

read

sing

build

write

school

house

bus

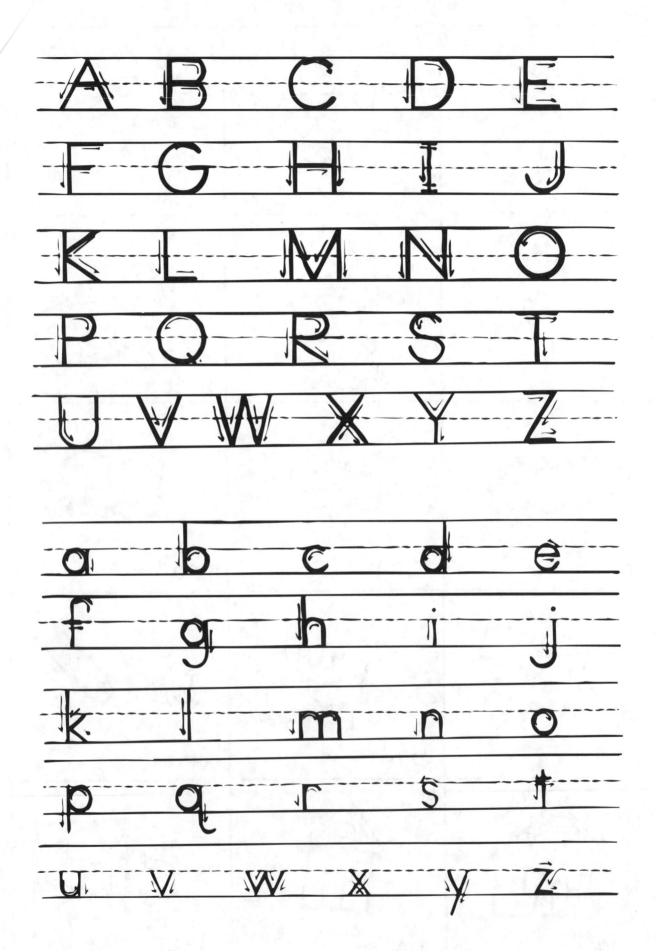

A B C D E
F G H I J
K L M N O
P Q R S T
U V W X Y Z

a b c d e
f g h i j
k l m n o
p q r s t
u v w x y z